Sober as F***

My Two Year Journey of Rediscovery & Self Love

Sarah Ordo

SOBER AS F***

Cover Art © Caroline Johnson

caroline-teagle.squarespace.com

Edited by Cara Lockwood

edit-my-novel.com

ISBN: 1546478329

ISBN-13: 978-1546478324

CONTENTS

To every little member of my dysfunctional, f***ed up sober family out there.
We got this.

1 | SOBER AS F***

There is a verse from 1 Corinthians 3:15 that took me aback the minute I heard it in church: "If it is burned up, the builder will suffer great loss but yet will be saved - even though only as one escaping the flames." There are certain times in your life when you hear or see something that strikes a chord in your heart and can shake you down to the darkest places of your soul. I sat alone in one of the aisles listening to the pastor preach that verse on that particular morning, sobbing. I was just over six months sober from alcohol, my boyfriend just left me two days before we were set to leave for a cruise for my birthday, and I had never felt so incredibly uncomfortable in the skin that covered every inch of my own body.

I clung to any and every fiber of strength in my body up until this point to hold myself together as I navigated this new sober life. I had no idea who I was anymore, I had no idea where my life was headed, and I had never felt so broken and so lost. I had finally broken. The pieces of the girl I used to be were shattered around me like shards of broken glass. It was like I had been trapped inside of a burning house yet managed to break through a window at the last possible second before it would have all collapsed on top of me... leaving my body and my soul to be burned up to ashes. I had suffered my great loss in many forms, just like the builder in the verse. And although I suffered those losses, I also had been saved. I'd endured a situation I should not have survived, I escaped through the flames of what my life had become.

I had always been very hesitant to call myself an "alcoholic" because I wasn't that person that woke up and had to have a drink. I was young, building my own business, had a lot of friends, and surely didn't resemble what I pictured an "alcoholic" would look like. Now I realize that every person's relationship with alcohol is not the same, and many people have broadly different issues with drinking. There is no cookie cutter definition for an "alcoholic"… You may be a daily alcoholic. You may be a weekend binger (like I was). You may be a secret drinker. You may finish every workday with a bottle of wine.

Alcohol can affect you in more ways physically, emotionally, and mentally than you can even fathom. And if you are someone out there reading this that has a healthy relationship with alcohol, none of this may apply to you. You may be fine having a glass of wine with dinner to simply unwind. You may enjoy an ice cold beer watching your favorite sporting event on the weekends. There are many of us that never had that kind of healthy relationship with alcohol, and some of us will be unable to ever have it. There is an alarming amount of people in the world that have this issue. They may be white, black, Asian, gay, straight, successful, struggling, and so on and so on. Drinking and substance abuse have become more prevalent now than they ever have been in society before. The number of deaths I've seen show up on my Facebook Timeline from drinking, drugs, and overdoses has been climbing at a staggering rate in the last few years. The millennial generation (mine) seems to be hit hardest, and it's time to shine some light on this growing epidemic. It needs to be addressed, and we need to talk about it.

With almost two years of sobriety under my belt now, I kept feeling like there was something more I was supposed to do with my sobriety to share it with others. I am a firm believer in the idea of receiving signs and direction from the Universe and from God, if you are open and willing to receive them. My blog, soberAF.com, was the first step I took in sharing my story through writing after initially sharing my videos about getting sober on YouTube. I received such a positive response to the videos and blog posts that I felt the stirring in my heart to do more.

People from all over the world emailed me with stories like mine. I received friend requests from people of all ages asking for advice. People of all races and backgrounds reached out to me, looking for someone to lean on for support and encouragement. Initially, I felt overwhelmed, but the outpouring of need made me realize that there were a lot of people battling the same demons I battled, and they wanted to talk about it. I became pen pals with several people, writing them on a regular basis from all different countries and all walks of life... A European man around my age that had a story and personality strikingly similar to mine... A newly-engaged young woman navigating her newly sober journey trying to plan a wedding without incorporating alcohol into it... A husband from the South who was having trouble with relapsing because of the friends and family around him... I then received an email from a broadcasting contact at Dateline NBC asking to feature a clip from my One Year Sober video from YouTube on national television. The stirring in my heart grew stronger and stronger with every reassurance or sign I received from the Universe. But I wasn't quite sure what more I could do.

I woke up the morning after my 28th birthday to a dream so vivid and so clear that there was no way I could possibly ignore it. I dreamt I found a book on the floor. I picked it up but still didn't have any idea what it was. As I opened it and flipped through the pages, I realized that the book I held in my hands was not just a random book, but that it was *my* book. The universe had just shown me what I was supposed to do loud and clear, and there was no way I was going to ignore it.

So here I am. I have never written a book, and frankly, I have no idea what the hell I'm doing. But I decided to just start writing... to let any and every part of my struggle, my journey, and my rebirth be shared by the chance that someone else may take comfort and hope from some part of it. I know that at times I felt so desperate for the support and comfort of seeing that there could be a light at the end of the tunnel. I needed to hear that success in sobriety was possible and that I could find my way there.

I want to offer you that reassurance. You can make it. Cutting something like alcohol or drugs out of your life after they have been a part of it for so long is freaking HARD, and I don't intend to sugar coat any part of it for you. Anyone can tell you that it takes an inner strength that you never even knew you were possible of harnessing inside of you. This story is my story. But it is not all about me, and it is not all about alcohol. The transformation I went through during the first 365 days of my sobriety and beyond is one that I sometimes find hard to put into words, but it has been nothing short of miraculous. It has been an overwhelming and emotional experience that has altered everything about me.

Every single aspect of my life is different now. While the title of this book relates to being sober as f*** from alcohol, it also refers to the sobering realities and realizations I faced along the way. Although the alcohol itself was a huge part of it, there was a lot more beneath the surface that contributed to the way I had been living my life.

I personally found that the emotional and mental transformations I went through were sometimes even more powerful than the urge to drink had ever been. Recovery and living sober have challenged me in ways I could have never dreamed of, and made me grow stronger day by day with every hurdle that I passed. I was forced to grow a serious pair of lady balls to deal with this one. I was forced to cut my life apart, to deal with the underlying issues I had drug behind me like a piece of carry-on luggage for so long, and to also realize what areas of my life I was responsible of changing for the better if I was going to make it. The rollercoaster of the first 365 days had so many ups and downs and yet, now I appreciate them so much. EVERYTHING CHANGED…More than I could have ever even imagined it would. And the 365 days that followed that first year were about completely rebuilding myself and my life in a way I never saw coming. And, oh, what a blessing it has been.

If you picked up this book or downloaded it onto your Kindle or iPad, there is a chance that maybe your story goes a little bit like mine did. You may already be starting down the road of your own rediscovery. You may already be sober (Woo hoo!) and proud of it. You may just absolutely love drinking yourself into a stupor on a regular basis and are looking for the strength to change your ways. You may be trying to figure out how to reach your own place of self love. If any of these descriptions fit your story in any way, I welcome you into mine with open arms. If I could make it down this rocky road then you certainly can too. xo.

2 | FROM THE BEGINNING

From a young age I was quite used to being the center of attention. I liked to be seen as "perfect," which we all know doesn't really exists. My mother always tied my long, perfectly curled hair back with perfectly tied little bows or headbands that coordinated with my perfect little outfits. It was just a part of my daily routine to be praised with "she's SO cute!" with people I met complimenting my hair and outfits when we went out. I was on stage performing ballet by the age of three, in my little pink tutu with my perfectly coiled bun on top of my head. I loved the lights, I loved the sparkly outfits, and I loved the roar of applause I would receive at the end of a performance. I guess you could say from a very young age I was raised to put myself out there on the stage of life for all to see. As I grew older, I can now look back and realize that I grew to crave this type of attention and approval throughout my entire young adult life. I always had to put myself out there in one way or another and I thrived off of the positive things that would be said about me in return.

My childhood was a good one, full of all the happy times, smiles, and laughs that any parent hopes to give to their child. We were spoiled with experiences, and my mother always did everything she could to make every day special for us. Okay, we were probably a little spoiled with material things as well, but we were never rich or had an overabundance of fancy things. She spent all summer with us at the pool, going shopping, taking trips, and any other fun childhood activities you could think of. My father was around when he was not working but he went up north a lot to our cottage, so we spent a lot more time with my mother regularly. I really can't complain about my childhood at all. It was easy and it was pleasant. It was simple and it was innocent. Sometimes I wish I could feel that way as an adult, but we all know growing up brings responsibilities and worry, and that's just a part of life.

As a preteen, I spent mornings making myself look absolutely perfect before my day at school began. Looking back, I was a little obsessive about it to be honest. I would redo my ponytail with a circle of butterfly clips around it as many times as I had to until it was absolutely perfect. I literally would be late for school, redoing my hair in tears if it had any little bumps or imperfections during the fourth grade. All that mattered to me was that I was getting the approval I felt like I so desperately needed from others at all times.

When I started to hit puberty and my body began to change, I obsessed over making sure I was still "skinny". Being in dance where we had to wear a leotard and tights daily only amplified my need to make sure I was still staying thin and excelling in the dance world. It literally got to points where I would only eat dry cereal until dinner to make sure I didn't gain any more weight than the other girls in my dance classes. This is a time when a lot of girls start to hit puberty, or their "awkward stage,"… but is it just me, or do girls today completely skip that stage altogether? It is unfair that todays preteens go straight to being Instagram ready and completely skip this awkward stage of figuring out how to dress for your changing body, and also how to attempt to start shaping your eyebrows and shaving your legs. It was a rite of passage, people!

I had attended a private Catholic school up until eighth grade, when I switched to a public school. I only knew a few people. I remember planning my outfit for the first day of school and waking up extra early so that I could put a little makeup on that my mom had given me from her Clinique Bonus Time Gift and make sure that my hair looked absolutely perfect, as usual. My first day went well, and I loved public school. I was somewhat popular right away, especially after one of the popular boys told people he wanted to be my "boyfriend" (if you can even consider that being an actual relationship in eighth grade). I was so excited that people had accepted and liked me in my new school.

Of course, nothing could be perfect forever. Things hit a few rough patches later that year. A bully that didn't like me shoved me into lockers and tried to fight me in the hallways numerous times. Then my "boyfriend" started rumors that we had messed around in a movie theatre and it spread around the entire school. I was absolutely mortified that people thought it was true. I had always focused so much on portraying my perfect little picture, and it was being torn apart by rumors about me flying through the hallways. I had no idea how to react or respond to this type of scenario, because I had never experienced it before.

This was the first time I really experienced depression. I did not know how to deal with this type of situation and all of the emotions that came flooding in. I wanted to quit dancing and I started listening to "Creep" by Radiohead about 30 times per day. I tried to cut myself with cuticle scissors in the bathroom on multiple occasions until someone at school noticed that I was hiding the cut marks under a bunch of silver bangle bracelets. If I was really trying to hurt myself, I could have at least used something sharper than cuticle scissors, but my twelve year-old self really had no idea what she was doing. I even remember one particular time taking about a dozen pain killers from the bathroom cabinet and swallowing them down.

I had nobody to talk to, or least that's how I felt at the time. I was embarrassed to tell my friends, I was scared for my family to know, and I hid all my real emotions behind a big, shiny smile. I couldn't dare let anyone know or see that the perfect little image I portrayed my life to be was anything but spotless and shiny. Did I really want to hurt or kill myself? Absolutely not. These were just my little screams for someone to give me the attention and approval that I had become so heavily dependent on throughout my life. I just wanted to be liked by everyone and I just wanted to feel loved…

I had always felt like somewhat of the "outsider child" in my family, even from a young age. My older brother always played it safe, and I was the polar opposite of that. My entire family plays it safe, actually, and I have always been the one to break the mold. I was a wild child, even when I was young. My preteen years were when my rebellious nature first began to surface. We would have sleepovers at friends' houses and sneak out to walk to CVS when we shouldn't have been out.

The first time I actually tried alcohol was in a friends basement using liquor from her parents' bar. We made "tequila sunrises" which to a bunch of twelve and thirteen year-old girls was orange juice with grenadine and just a splash of whatever hard liquor was available in their bar. We definitely didn't drink anywhere near enough to feel a buzz, but we told everyone at school the next day thinking that we were SO cool. I wanted people to think I was cool and I wanted that attention on myself. This was my first taste of being seen as someone that was wild, cool, and breaking the rules, and I felt like others at school were envious of my life. Who knows if they actually were, but I was thriving off this type of feeling big time. I began to associate being popular with having my name be a part of the gossip and the buzz, which just reinforced my rebellious behavior tenfold. If I was the one behaving in ways that would fuel the rumors, I felt that I somewhat had control of what others were thinking or saying about me.

High school for me was an absolute breeze most of the time. I was pretty popular and got above average grades. I was in yearbook, a handful of extra curricular activities and clubs, and on the Homecoming Court smiling big with that sash draped across my absolutely perfect dress on the football field. I was a party girl, to say the least. Most photos taken of myself during this time were decorated with a bottle or a drink in my hand constantly. Every weekend we would all carpool over to whoever's house was empty, or whoever parents didn't care if we drank in the basement. I had had my first drink the summer before high school, when we raided that friend of mine's parents bar to make those tequila sunrises that probably didn't intoxicate us at all... But in high school I was drunk all weekend, every weekend. I always had a half empty carton of Marlboro Lights in my Saturn Twin Cab center console at all times. Any event wasn't complete without a pregame plan of where we would drink vodka out of water bottles and smoke cigarettes beforehand. Any and every event just became an excuse to show up being drunk and loud in my perfectly coordinated outfit for everyone to see.

I was handed a ticket for being a Minor in Possession of Alcohol at the age of sixteen, but I couldn't even tell you how many times I had run from the cops throughout those four years. I became quite the pro at jumping fences to run away from the police while wearing a destroyed Hollister denim mini skirt. That ticket at the age of sixteen bought me a hefty fine to pay, hundreds of community service hours, six months of reporting probation with a probation officer, and one extremely awkward "Abusive Addictions" class to complete. Just picture several teenagers in their varsity jackets surrounded by felons in folding metal chairs watching videos about people whose addictions had ruined their lives. Judging by how my years following that class would go, it did absolutely nothing to scare me away from drinking.

You know that my parents were PISSED as hell about my getting that ticket. I could feel the strain become real between us after this screw up. I'm shocked I didn't get into more legal trouble throughout my teenage years, honestly. Any and every event became a reason to "pregame" with friends. I even attended my senior prom with a plastic cell phone shaped flask of vodka strapped to my garter on my upper thigh. Classy, I know.

Looking back, high school was definitely my gateway to experimenting with everything unhealthy. I thought, like everyone at this age, that I was absolutely invincible. Everyone I knew was trying things and behaving poorly, so I just followed suit. I liked people talking about me at school, it made me feel important. The wilder I acted, the more attention I got. At least I was the one in control of what was being said about me by doing this, right? I think this conditioned me for the out-of-control party animal I grew to be in the coming years. The crazier I would act, the more attention I would get... so if I got absolutely shit faced in a slutty outfit every weekend I would surely get a ton of attention.

Of course, high school wasn't just partying. I fell in love for the first time, too, and he cheated on me numerous times along the way. This definitely contributed to the beginning of the issues I would have with men for years to come, even after I had stopped partying.

Between the end of high school and when I started college was probably one of the last times I was really somewhat stable and in control of myself and my life. Call it the calm before the storm, but shit really started to get crazier after I turned eighteen years old. I wasn't even legally old enough to drink, and I had already experimented with more things than some people do in their entire lifetime. Weekend after weekend was a blur of alcohol, drugs, guys, and piecing back together the nights I didn't have one memory of when I woke up somewhere other than my own bed the following morning.

My relationship with my family had become even more strained at this point. Any father would hate to see his daughter going down the road I was going down, and being that he did not drink at all, I'm sure it was even more difficult for him to digest. My poor mother tried to hold on to me, but I'm sure I made it extremely difficult for her to do so. She tried to keep the friendship we had shared when I was young, but sometimes when I look back I wish she would have tried to control me a little bit more and be my friend a little bit less. But then again, I was the badass, rebellious child so I probably wouldn't have listened to her anyways even if she had tried. My brother and I grew farther apart during this time, and I'm not surprised. Who would want to have the little sister known for being drunk at every event and being the party girl at school? We had always been a little different, but now it almost seemed like we weren't related at all. My family's opposition to my ways just made me want to do them more, but also made me feel like the outcast at the same time. There were moments when I felt that they didn't expect much from me anymore, and had lost faith in my future.

College just became an amplified version of my high school party girl status. I joined a sorority and this just fueled my behavior even more. Every weekend I'd head to a frat party where I'd pass out on one of the couches with another sorority sister around four in the morning. I remember thinking it was hilarious that I would come to frat parties with my own half gallon of Five O' Clock Vodka and drink it without a chaser. I would literally drink straight from my half gallon bottle of the cheapest vodka possible, and it smelled like a combination of straight up rubbing alcohol and gasoline. People would laugh and encourage me as I got more and more wasted and the rest of the evening would just be a complete blackout. On sorority semi-formal night, my sisters and date had to carry me onto my parents' porch, unconscious after I didn't even make it past the bus ride to the event.

Waking up in weird places became my staple. I woke up on couches and would stumble over to the fridge to see if my friends and I could figure out whose house we'd passed out in by looking at the pictures stuck on it. Although it sounds like an absolute mess, it was my lifestyle of being a lush and an absolute mess that needed all of the attention at all times. I loved the mess, I loved the chaos. I loved telling people all about my crazy stories of being drunk, and the attention I received from them made me feel like I was just the coolest person around town. I felt like people were envious of my life, when they really probably just thought I was out of control.

I was so blinded by the need to feel "cool" and popular by others, and I would do anything to keep that image. I plastered photos of myself and all my "party girl" friends all over Facebook every weekend to show everyone how fun my life was. It was a great way for me to cover up and drown away all of the insecurities and emotions that I didn't want to face or deal with. I simply hid them away and never dealt with them, one swig of vodka at a time.

I knew I had issues. Many times I should've heeded the wake-up calls in my life in my early twenties. People I cared for lost respect for me. I ripped my chin open from someone letting me go face first into the concrete in a parking lot while they were holding me up unconsciously drunk. I had taken so much Molly one night that I was still high well into the next day. I literally had to tell myself to break at every red light while driving to the salon where I worked, or else I wouldn't have remembered to do so. I repeatedly had to call credit card companies to cancel all of my cards after having my wallet stolen while wasted. I was so messed up from someone putting something in my drink at a New Years Eve party in Flint, MI that I literally could not push myself up with all my might from the couch I was laying on to get away from a random guy that was trying to make a move on me. Another guy I knew at the party walked in and saw what was happening. The memory is extremely hazy, but I remember that he was yelling at the guy to stop and screaming "What the f*** are you doing!?" while throwing him out of the room. The partial memory I have of this horrible night is one that I have only recently been able to face, accept, and move past ten years later.

Yet after every one of these horrible situations, I still convinced myself that I didn't need to change, that my extreme ways made me look cool and made others envy my lifestyle. I told myself everyone wished their life was like mine. I thought that surely I was having more fun and living my days to their full potential, one party at a time. I thought that I was the shit, and that everyone wanted my life.

Chaos and my life were like two magnetic objects that just could not stay away from each other. I got kicked out of my student teaching placement towards the end of college for something I posted on Facebook with profanity. I totaled my car in Detroit at 2 am when I got off work from gogo dancing at an EDM nightclub, and then the driver of the other car tried to jump me. Thankfully, it was closing time and a group of guys standing outside a bar were able to huddle me into a doorway and block me with their bodies from the girls trying to swing at me. My mother had begged me for months to stop working in downtown Detroit on late weekend nights, but I didn't care. She would stay up until 3 am to talk to me on the phone to make sure I got to my car safe and was driving home. A guy I met while online dating keyed the word "WOHRE" into the side of my car in my own backyard after I left mid-date when he got drunkenly loud and aggressive (that's right, he spelled 'whore' wrong). I almost got sued when my addict ex-boyfriend abandoned the house we were renting together and absolutely trashed it. These are just a few examples of what my life was typically like. I never considered the consequences of anything while I was doing it.

All I was concerned about was myself. I was selfish, narcissistic, and in denial about it completely. As long as I was having a good time, it didn't matter in my mind that I was living out my own self-destructive patterns over and over again everywhere I went. My life was a whirlwind of absolute chaos, always one thing after another after another, and never still for long enough for me to face my real underlying problems. The chaos became safe in that way: it helped me hide from my real issues.

What was it about this lifestyle that was so attractive to me? I cannot honestly give a confident, whole-hearted answer to that question, because I don't really know what it was about it that I enjoyed so much. Surely the attention I received was just fuel to my fire. I had gotten into the routine of looking good and getting smashed every weekend. Did this show that I was successful? Did this show that I was happy? Not at all.

The funny thing was that I always felt a little uncomfortable when I was drunk but at the point that I was fully aware of things and not blacked out yet. I didn't like feeling like I was unable to control myself, so I would simply drink more to get past that stage. I didn't like the feeling of not being able to come out of whatever high

I was feeling, or feeling like I couldn't control myself… HUGE RED FLAG. But obviously I didn't pay any attention to it. Most people would stop at the point that they felt uncomfortable, but my addictive personality told me to just keep going to get past it.

I loved the party, I loved dancing, I loved laughing with my friends, and I loved meeting new people. In my mind being absolutely wasted while doing these things just made them even more fun and amplified my good time, when in reality I barely remembered any of it at all.

Somehow I was successful in school and always held a steady job. Regardless of my party lifestyle, I had always been able to hold it together extremely well in the career aspect of my life. Around 2013, I had the idea to start my business 24Luxe Hair & Makeup, an on-location hair and makeup traveling team. I licensed my LLC and worked my ass off to be successful with it from day one. I had always been an overachiever when it came to my career. At one point in my twenties, I was attending cosmetology school full time, taking night classes at the University of Michigan, and working as the receptionist and closer at a beauty salon all simultaneously. I was so busy everyday that I had no time to relax, and when I did it was usually a weekend night and I headed straight for the bottle to let loose.

My parents had told me no when I suggested that I wanted to stop attending college and go to beauty school instead, and I distinctly remember being so angry at them that I was lying in bed with tears in my eyes. I told them "watch me" and soon after applied for my first loan to sign up for beauty school. Telling me I couldn't do something just made me just want to do it even more. It was basically a challenge in my mind, so I had told myself that I would do this just to prove them wrong. So I did it. I finished beauty school, I graduated from college, and I worked in a beauty salon on the weekends while I taught Preschool during the week with my Early Childhood degree. I loved the kids, and I loved my job, but my heart was still in the beauty industry. This was when I quit teaching and started my business, and it was one of the best decisions of my life.

I began making YouTube videos and making a little bit of money off of social media on the side. I also worked at a cosmetic counter part-time waxing, because I loved being busy. Being busy made me feel good because it made me feel like I was kicking ass at something, even if I was a mess in all the other areas of my life. Receiving praise from others for my success and drive just fueled my desire to be even more successful. People encouraged and applauded me for starting my own thing and chasing after my dreams, and it made me feel so good. I loved seeing my business grow knowing that I was the one making it happen. My passion for the beauty industry always kept me focused and determined to be successful above everything else because I did truly love what I was doing. I often threw myself into my work when other things weren't going smoothly because at least I was still doing that one thing right in my life. I couldn't have lost all control if I was still being successful in my work, right? This was what I convinced myself over and over again... That I couldn't possibly be an "alcoholic" because look at how well I was doing in my career.

I have realized over time that I have a somewhat "addictive" personality in all aspects of life. When I like something, I want it... and I want a lot of it. I can see now that I practiced this in all areas of life. In relationships, I would spend an unhealthy amount of time with someone if I really liked (or even loved) them. If I enjoyed a television show or movie, I would binge watch it. If I had an idea or a goal, I obsessed over it and worked on it relentlessly.

Things I was passionate about or enjoyed I would become somewhat obsessed with, but never in an alarming way. I can only assume that this is part of the reason I would binge drink. I loved partying, and I loved doing a lot of it. I wouldn't just have a few drinks when I went out, I would keep going until the bar closed down... and then I would just continue drinking at whoever's place I ended up at after that.

I had to go out every weekend. My life got busier with my business growing, and I didn't always have a ton of free time. So on the weekend I would wake up at the crack of dawn (or sometimes earlier) to do bridal makeup, work all day, get ready and pregame drink, and go out because I saw it as my "release" that I had earned after a busy week. I could let go of all my cares and just party and have fun. I had deserved it by working so hard, right? I was so busy a lot of the time that when I did party, I would party HARD. I had so much stress and work during the other days that I felt this was my chance to party it all away for a night or two, to let all my cares go to the wind for just a little while.

As far as relationships, I think I may have had one or two men in my life that I would consider to be "healthy" relationships, but most were not. I was drawn to those men that I wanted to fix. People always told me that I "dated down" when it came to guys, and maybe they were right. I always tried to give everyone the benefit of the doubt and had hope that deep down inside everyone was basically a good person. While this can be an amazing quality for people to have, it can also lead to a lot of hurt and pain along the way. I was naïve, and I just wanted someone to love me and pay attention to me.

Guys with addictions, guys with baby mamas, guys with shitty jobs and no drive to excel in life… these were the ones that gave me all of the attention I thought I needed. It may have been because I was too good for them, and none of them showed anywhere near what I deserved from a significant other in return. I don't say this to sound cocky or like I am full of myself, but if you saw many of these men and heard the stories of our relationships you would absolutely agree with me one hundred percent. Meanwhile, I gave them my whole heart. I did at least get my adorable chihuahua Kaya out of one of my first unhealthy relationships. She is my little baby and I love her, oh, SO much.

I was hurt numerous times by the people who told me they loved me, and I began to lose faith and the ability to trust in people in general. I had made the men in my life into what Gabrielle Bernstein refers to in her book *Spirit Junkie* as "idols." I was staying in relationships with people that I knew weren't right for me just to have someone around. I put these men above myself as if they were some type of idol that I felt I needed to have around to make things okay in my own life.

I definitely struggled with some major codependency issues over the years. I always had to have someone around to make myself feel worthy and good enough. I had to be wanted by someone to feel complete. Of course that was all just something I had convinced myself in my head, but I wasn't able to see that until years later.

Having someone that wanted and desired me reassured me that I was still the good-looking, perfect young woman I so desperately wanted to be seen as at all times. While I constantly felt the need to have a relationship to feel complete, I also became dangerously talented at subduing my feelings. I became extremely good at shutting off the things I didn't want to feel and the emotions that came along with them, because it was much easier to numb it with a drink or twelve rather than to actually deal with them after each heartbreak and disappointment. I became very able to disconnect my feelings from people. It is frightening how quickly I was able to mentally cut off the last guy and start looking for the next. I would shed about five tears, post some bullshit motivational quote on Instagram about being a "strong, independent woman," and immediately look for the next guy. I would get wasted and party to get over things, and meet a new guy while I was wasted to avoid dealing with the emotions from the last one. I was literally just shoveling all of the bullshit and baggage from one relationship into the next.

In my mid-twenties, one of my friends moved to downtown Detroit. We had such a blast being able to walk to a ton of cool restaurants, bars, and events every weekend. It was so exciting being in a downtown area and having so many things to go do together all the time. This also meant that nobody had to drive… which you can only imagine just fueled us to down even more shots at the bar when guys offered them to us. I started seeing a guy towards the end of my partying who was coincidentally several years sober. I waved to him on his motorcycle on my way downtown to my friend's place, and we exchanged numbers. I invited him to meet us at the bar that night. When he didn't order a drink I asked him why and he explained that he was several years sober. He had had issues with both alcohol and drugs before hitting rock bottom, but was quite proud of his recovery. I convinced my friends multiple times that I "couldn't seriously date an ex-addict." All I cared about was that I met him while he was riding a motorcycle and that he was hot with a ton of tattoos... typical me.

Every single weekend became a pregame, followed by drinking as much as we could at the bar, stumbling back, and then polishing off any bottles of wine left in the fridge. I would wake up the next morning on her couch, eat a McDonald's breakfast sandwich in my car during my still intoxicated drive home, pull myself together, and go work a wedding doing bridal makeup without anyone even knowing about the debauchery that had gone down the night before. Thankfully, I think I received my grandfather's alcoholic genes because I never missed a wedding job. I was never even late to a wedding we were working because I had been partying the night before. While everyone else was hungover and feeling like death, I simply woke up and kept going. I prided myself on it, but now when I think about it, it just makes me realize that I was basically a major "functioning alcoholic" in the form of a weekend binge drinker.

I won't elaborate too much on this stage of my life because looking back I was acting in ways that make me cringe at the amount of alcohol I was consuming and the choices I made while I was that wasted out of my mind. I would say things, do things, and go places that I would never do sober. This was what ultimately led me into all of the chaos I always found myself falling into. My judgement was completely out the window while I was blackout drunk. Most people pass out, but not me. I'd walk around in a black-out state, fully functioning still. That was an extremely dangerous setup of factors, as you can imagine. I wouldn't remember one glimmer of the night yet I would go to multiple bars, clubs, or parties. People would say they saw me somewhere, and I wouldn't even remember being there.

They would be shocked when I told them this and insist they talked to me and I "didn't even seem that drunk", while I didn't even remember seeing them at all.

I will just say that I truly cannot believe I didn't end up seriously hurt, with some sort of disease, or in the hospital sooner. I believe someone or something was looking out for me. There was no other way to explain it. There were so many times I had been so careless and put myself in so many situations where things could have gone very, very wrong. I like to think now that maybe God was looking out for me and conjuring up the big thing he would throw my way to finally make me have my wake up call. I also like to think that whatever higher powers there are in the Universe were aligning things up just right to keep me safe along the way so I could reach my turning point. I find reassurance in believing that friends and people I have lost along the way were watching over me as guardian angels every step along the way.

All I know is that there were hundreds of times something could have happened and something should have gone wrong. I was playing with fire with my own life pretty much every weekend. I felt invincible and never thought that anything would stop me from living every day of my life pushing it to the edge of almost losing everything. I was young, I was successful, and I was thriving off of this lifestyle I had built for myself. I was going harder and harder with my drinking and partying with every weekend that passed, and I saw no end in sight.

I had always done everything in my life to an excess, and I thrived off of pushing boundaries and challenging limits. I was now pushing and pushing against the tipping point of losing all control. This was just the perfect storm brewing that would ultimately lead to the day that would change my life forever. God was just setting up the chain of events that would follow once I finally pushed hard enough to cause everything to come crumbling and crashing down around me. On a day I had no idea would change my life forever, I pushed against that wall one more time, and it would all come crashing down on me all at once.

3 | MAY 24TH-25TH 2015

I had on my favorite pair of destroyed, high rise, bleached out jeans with a tight cropped top so that a decent amount of my abs and skin were showing. I was wearing my favorite platform flip flops that boosted my five foot figure in the height department just a little bit more. My hair was in perfect messy curls and my makeup and lashes looked flawless. One of my girlfriends had come over to get ready and pregame before we headed to downtown Detroit for a music festival. My pregame consisted of taking some Aderall followed by three quarters of a fifth of tequila mixed with margarita mix in a massive insulated mason jar. I was so excited to be wasted out of my mind, look awesome in my outfit, and dance the night away with my friends downtown to the best EDM music. We looked forward to this music festival every year because we always stayed out all hours of the night and did some of the craziest partying we would do all year.

I took a few selfies in the bathroom before we left to drive downtown. The perfectly put together girl looking out from those selfies had no idea what was about to happen. The selfie that I posted on Instagram that day will forever cause my stomach to drop to the floor whenever I see it for the rest of my life. I didn't know it at that time, but it could have been the last picture ever taken of me alive.

Once we arrived and realized we were going to be waiting in line for hours to get our tickets, I quickly made friends with the guys in line behind us when they said they were going to walk to the liquor store. That's the kind of girl I was. I would use my looks and my charm to get alcohol from guys so I wouldn't have to buy it myself. I came back with a pint of Smirnoff Vodka under my arm along with a 40 ounce of Mike's Hard Lemonade to wash it down with.

Needless to say, I don't remember anything beyond finishing that combination of alcohol on top of what I had already consumed during my pregame. From what others told me (since I was completely blacked out at this point), I finished all of my alcohol and also shared some of whatever the people in front of me had to drink afterward. My friend told me that she had stopped me at one point before we got inside to ask if I was okay, but I assured her I was fine and just having fun. I apparently also bought another mixed drink once we finally got inside the festival, which I'm assuming I finished as well. What I am going to tell you from this point forward is what I was told by my friends, medical personnel, and doctors as they pieced back together an evening I had absolutely no recollection of at all until I woke up in the Emergency Room several hours later.

I was dancing around without a care in the world to the beats of the music, and talking to a handsome guy with long hair and a backpack. We were laughing and whispering things back and forth, and my friend said she thought we were making out when she first looked over. The next thing she knew, she was watching him shovel a handful of pills of some sort into my mouth. I'd like to elaborate at this point that I had always been against taking pills or things from people that I didn't know. I was never one to take things from a complete stranger on the dance floor at a show or party. I never liked feeling so under the influence of something that I could not pull myself out of, even though I was usually so drunk already that I was never able to realize it anyways. I only took things from people that I knew or were a trusted source. I was always worried that I was going to get something cut with another drug or something dangerous. I had heard horror stories of people getting bad pills or things cut with something that made them sick, so I was always a psycho to make sure I knew exactly what I was getting.

It's funny to think about how I thought I was being so careful by looking out for myself and what I took, when I was really just drinking myself into a stupor and taking drugs recreationally all the time. My reason for explaining this is to elaborate that sober I would have never taken a handful of random pills from someone that I did not know. Even though I liked having a good time, I was always careful about that for some odd reason. But once I was blacked out, obviously my decision making skills were non-existent... So down the hatch that handful off pills had gone.

About fifteen minutes later, I turned around, grabbed a friend of ours by the front of his T-shirt, and collapsed to the ground. He carried me over to a grassy area where I heaved a few times so they gave me water, thinking that I just needed to throw up. I stood up and immediately collapsed again to the concrete where my eyes began rolling back into my head. One of my friends had gone to college as a dental assistant, and had basic medical training, so she kept checking for my pulse, and noticed it was getting more and more faint.

I can only imagine how panicked they must have felt at this moment. The guy with us ran me towards the front of the festival carrying my almost lifeless body in his arms through the crowds. My friend told me she could hear him yelling "I'm not letting her die in my arms..." over and over again while he ran carrying me. After they got me to the medical tent, I was behind a curtain for about five or ten minutes until the nurse told my friends that I was being taken by ambulance to the nearest Emergency Room in Detroit. I vaguely remember a flash of a memory from my blackout, but I could tell that I was being held down either by someone or tied down by straps, which I will probably never know which one it was. They wouldn't let anyone come in the ambulance with me that was not family, so I don't have a concrete story of what happened before we made it to the hospital. I can recall a women's voice that kept repeating very loudly, "What did you take, sweetie?" over and over. I remember trying to pull myself up and being able to feel that I was being held down from my chest. The woman in the ambulance kept telling me to stop and asking what I took, but that was all I remembered at all from that portion of the night.

According to the nurses and doctors, my body had been shutting down in response to an extremely high blood alcohol level in combination with a "lethal cocktail" of MDMA and Ketamine in my system. Just to elaborate on what that means, Ketamine is commonly used as a horse tranquilizer… Yeah.

At some point I began to have a seizure and bit partially into my tongue. My heart rate was at an elevated rate to the point that I had to be monitored with EKG censors all over my chest to make sure I didn't have a stroke or go into cardiac arrest for hours. One of my friends came to the hospital to make sure I was okay. She said that when she got there I kept talking about "bright light" and saying people looked like "angels." I don't remember her getting there at all. They told her I had to stay at the hospital until all of my vitals were monitored and back to normal levels again, so she sat next to my hospital bed in tears and stayed with me.

I was still so messed up out of my mind that I was asking nurses for makeup brushes and turkey bacon. I even told a male nurse to "find my name on your charts and add me on Facebook… because I'm not usually like this" (We laughed about this afterwards, because how could you not?). I was screaming out to other patients asking what was wrong with them. When they brought me my clothes to get dressed, I asked the nurse if I had taken my clothes off in front of everyone, but she reassured me that they had undressed me while I was unconscious upon my arrival to get me into a hospital gown. These nurses and doctors must have surely hated me at this point. People were at the hospital with serious medical issues, and here I was almost killing myself with something like partying. I then quickly realized that I had no shoes, my backpack was not with me, and I had no idea where my money, ID, and car keys were.

A doctor basically told me at one point, "You shouldn't be alive right now, but somehow you are. You pulled through when your body was literally shutting down on itself." Initially, I nodded and told him that I understood, but at that time I wasn't able to fully grasp the reality of what had just happened at all. I was still extremely messed up from the insane cocktail of things I had taken that night.

So I walked out of the ER barefoot, with a $3,000 hospital bill on the way (that would not be covered by my shitty health insurance), makeup running down my face, insisting to my friend that we go to the after-hours party to go find the friends I had been with because hopefully they had all of my belongings. She refused (thankfully), and took me to her neighbors apartment where the guys that lived below her forced me to stay there and cooked pizza rolls for me so I had something in my stomach. The friends I had been with eventually answered their phones around 7 am and said that they had my car and were coming to get me.

I will forever be grateful for the friend that came to the hospital to stay with me and took me to her place when I was discharged. No matter what life may have done to our relationship or how far we have grown apart now, I could never thank her enough for being there on that day when nobody else was.

I could never apologize enough to Sarah and Christie, the sisters that I had grown up with that lived across the street when I was younger. One of the friends I was with had called Sarah knowing that she would be able to get in touch with my mom. She called my mom while she was up north at our cottage and Sarah was the one that had to explain to her that her daughter was in the hospital in Detroit but that she had no idea what had happened beyond that.

Sarah and I have grown into very different women over the years. She has always been an amazing person. She is kind, she is selfless, and she has a heart of gold. Although we were polar opposites from our late teens to mid-twenties, she never turned her back on me. There was even an occasion where Sarah left church on a Sunday morning to take her Dad's car and pick me up as I sat on a curb in my outfit from the night before in front of a guy's apartment

27

where I'd passed out. If that doesn't describe our everlasting friendship through our differences, I don't know what else does. She has always been there for me no matter how much of a mess I've become or made in my life. I stood on the altar with her when she got married, and I will have her standing by me whenever I find my husband in life. I appreciate Sarah and her sister Christie for never turning their backs on me, and I apologize to them so deeply for putting them in the position to break the news to my mother on that night.

I got home the morning of May 25th, 2015 around 7 am after my friends dropped me off and I tried to sleep a little, but wasn't really able to at all. Nothing had completely hit me or registered yet. I remember tossing and turning for hours, still messed up from everything I had in my system from the night before. Those several hours in bed were extremely hazy and all melted together, and I didn't even feel like I was fully there. I continuously replayed what had happened over and over again, and was beginning to process more and more of what had just happened. I just kept thinking that if I could fall asleep I would wake up and feeling this way would go away. I was so tired and all I wanted was to sleep, but that wasn't going to happen at all right now.

I went over to my mom's house that afternoon. She had been up north when all of this had happened, and I can only imagine how it felt to be a mother hours away from home and getting a phone call with hardly any cell phone service saying her daughter had been rushed to the Emergency Room at Detroit Receiving Hospital.

Knowing my mother… it breaks my heart to think about how she must have felt and reacted in that moment. She was hours away on vacation and couldn't get to her baby girl. She loves her children more than anything else in life, and the thought of causing her such pain and worry is something I cannot even fathom. She held me when I walked in the door that morning, and I broke down completely.

I remember trying to nap in her bed while she sat in the chair next to it watching TV. Any time I would start to fall asleep I was having these little spasms where my leg would kick or my body would jump (side effects of everything I had taken, I'm sure), and like I was still her little baby she would immediately reach over and make sure I was okay. It was just like I'd seen my friends do when they were first time mothers to their newborn babies, checking to see if they are still breathing every hour their first few weeks of life because you are absolutely terrified something will be wrong with them at all times. I never knew the true extent of a mother's love for her child until that day. She could have been so angry with me that she wouldn't have even wanted to look at me, but instead she stayed right by my side the entire time. I was her broken and hurting 26-year-old baby girl, and she stayed with me through every minute of it. If anything, I knew I had to do something about what had happened simply because of what I had just put her through. She didn't deserve this, and something had to change.

My mom had told me that I should apologize to my older brother because he had been extremely upset by what had happened. I remember walking downstairs as tears started to well up in my eyes. My brother and I hadn't been very close in years, probably because we were polar opposites of each other. He always played it safe, was dedicated to school and his career, and did everything by the book. I, on the other hand, was the wild child of the family which I'm sure he hated while we were teenagers in the same high school. I struggled to get out an "I'm sorry" without letting my voice break up while I held back the tears. I was standing not even five feet away from him and he wouldn't even look at me. I have never felt like a bigger piece of shit in my life. I have never felt so small, so pathetic, so ashamed. He wouldn't even look at me. I walked away as I completely broke down into tears. I had hurt my own family, the people that have stood by my side through everything, to the point that they couldn't even look at me anymore.

The entire first day after everything happened I felt like I was just going through the motions. I don't remember many other significant things from this day. I just remember feeling numb... like nothing mattered. I had made phone calls to a few people and sent a few messages apologizing to Sarah and Christie, the sisters that had gotten a hold of my mom and tried to piece together what was going on that night. I thanked them for everything and explained how embarrassed and ashamed I was. I promised them I was going to do something about it, that I was going to change.

This was a turning point for me, and I realized how much I hated feeling this way. I knew I had to take some major responsibility for what I had done this time. I couldn't just laugh it off as another one of my crazy partying stories I bragged about to everyone for days after. This one was big, and it could have taken everything away from me. It could have taken a daughter away from her mother, a sister away from a brother, and a best friend away from a friend. I hated being in a position where I felt so terrible about myself and terrible about how I had affected others that cared about me. I had never felt like such an absolute loser as I did in that moment. I decided that day that something needed to change. I had been in enough situations already that should have opened my eyes and woken me up to the reality that I needed to grow up and change the way I lived my life.

I just couldn't put together how I had gotten here...How had I let myself get to this point? When had the fun-filled nights of partying gotten to the point that I had lost all control? I was so ashamed, so embarrassed, and I felt terrible for what I had put the people that cared about me through. Looking back, I can't believe that I had to almost lose my life and wake up in a hospital with all kinds of IVs and monitors hooked onto me to come to this realization. But some people just have to learn the hard way I guess, and I am one of them. You could have told me a million times I was going to end up hurt or dead before this and I would have continually brushed it off and thought you were just exaggerating. I would have told my mother she was being too overprotective every time she told me she stayed up all hours of the night worried about me. I was invincible, and nothing like that was ever going to happen to me… But then it did. Stubborn people sometimes don't learn the lessons they need to learn until it is front on them plain as day and they hit their rock bottom. I had surely just hit mine.

I thought about the idea many times that I had been pulled through something I shouldn't have survived, and that someone or something had surely been watching over me. Even if someone hadn't really been watching over me, I had made it through for some reason. I very well could have died that night, but I didn't. My time on this earth could have been up, but for some reason it was not. The idea that I had made it was enough to tell me that it was my time to not only surrender, but to rebuild. I had been given this second chance for some reason, and I would be a fool to take it for granted.

Why had I been saved? What was the purpose of me still being alive? I started to think about this idea on a much more spiritual level, and I had convinced myself deep in my heart that I had to do something to acknowledge this idea that I was still here for some divine reason. So I made the decision right then and there that I was going to change and make my life into something better. I was no longer going to throw away every day I was grateful enough to have left on this Earth with alcohol and partying. I was no longer going to be careless with the relationships of people that cared about me. I was going to turn this life of mine around in any and all ways possible. I decided that I would use this experience as the starting point to create a better life, the life that I deserved to live.

When you hit your rock bottom, you run out of any and all options of what to do next. You either have hit the point where your life will flash "game over" or you climb yourself back out of the lowest place you have fallen to. Rock bottom is a hopeless spot where all you can do if you want to move forward is surrender to whatever forces have put you there, and so I finally chose to surrender. I felt that I didn't have many other options at this point . I either would continue to live the way I had been living or change it, and I refused to give in and accept failure. As was with many things in my life, I never made failure an option for myself and I never took no for an answer. The idea that all the factors were against me in turning my life around was almost taunting me like a challenge, and you know I can't ever say no to a challenge. I decided once again that I would do the things I was told were unlikely and I would be unable to do on my own.

This was the day I decided to become sober. I wasn't sure how I was going to do it or what it was going to be like, but I said that I was going to stop drinking and I meant it. Being the stubborn, hard-headed girl that I am, I gave myself no option to fail at this new challenge in my life. I intended on going full steam ahead towards the bigger and better version of myself. I really had no idea what I was getting myself into, but I had told myself that I would do it no matter what. I wanted to defy all odds and become a success story. I wanted to challenge the norm and completely walk away from alcohol on my own. At this point I was so eager to successfully complete this new challenge I had given myself that I hadn't thought ahead at all about what this would mean. I hadn't thought about the difficulties I would face in changing everything about the life I had known for so long. A fire had been lit inside of me with a new challenge looking me dead in the face, and I was staring down right back at it.

I felt strong and fearless, and I was empowered by the idea of how I thought I was going to absolutely kill it when it came to changing my life. It would be easy for me is exactly what I was thinking at this point, because I was clueless about what I was walking into.

The idea of the way people would look at me differently was something that just drove me to want to do this even more. Just as I had always been desperate for the approval and praise of others, I knew that if I did this I would surely receive those things once again. I wasn't thinking about the type of self-satisfaction and pride I would feel inside myself by doing this, because I had always relied on getting these things from outside forces in my life. That is a whole other topic we will cover later on in the story, but at this point I was still looking outward for all of the things I thought would make me feel whole and feel better as a person. The idea that people would praise me and see me being successful at something in my life again was still fueling the fire quite a bit for me.

This decision to change everything on May 25th, 2015 has been the best decision I have ever made in my life. Although what was going to come next was going to be the hardest thing I've ever had to do, I was ready to face it. Really I had no other option but to face it, because I had given myself no option but to follow through on my decision regardless of what it took. I was going to be sober from alcohol, no matter what happened, because I simply refused to let myself fail or give up on the second chance I had been so lucky to receive.

I walked into this battle with my head held high and with a new type of determination in my heart. I was ready for war. What I didn't know was that the war I was about to face was going to take on many forms and shapes that I had no idea were even possible. This journey wasn't going to just be about cutting alcohol out of my life, it was going to be about rebuilding my life from the ground up. Every single thing was about to change and tear my world apart, and I had no freaking clue that I was strapping myself into the front row of the biggest roller coaster ride I would ever go on in my life.

4 | NAIVE & BROKEN

The first few days that followed were a blur of tears amid a literal emotional breakdown. The first time I went back to my apartment after staying at my mom's house, I walked in to see all of my things and it hit me hard right at that moment. Because if I had died, someone else would be standing in my doorway, looking to pack up my things... Every framed photo, the grocery list I had scribbled on the fridge, my mail stacked on the table... All of it could have been left just like it was for someone to pick through, throw away, or decide what mementos they wanted to keep to remember me by. I was not ready to grasp the heaviness of this idea yet, and it paralyzed me. The thought of my mother having to come to my place to go through her dead daughter's things was enough to break my heart to pieces instantly. I sat right there on the floor by the door and cried hysterically on and off for hours without moving.

Grasping the idea that I could have not made it out of the hospital alive was emotionally and mentally much harder for me than I thought it would be. For days and even weeks afterward I found myself noticing little moments and details of my daily life more than I ever had before. I found myself getting extremely emotional about how overwhelming it sometimes felt. I was over appreciative for my morning coffee on my townhouse balcony. The watermelon chunks I cut up tasted better than I ever remember watermelon tasting before.

I sat and enjoyed the morning a few minutes longer than I normally would with my long haired Chihuahua sitting on my lap. I noticed how extra blue the sky looked filled with white, fluffy clouds. It was like I was on some sort of sensory overload at all times for a while. I've read things online that say that when your body rids itself of alcohol, your senses can sometimes feel stronger because it can damper them when you drink a lot. Maybe this is what was happening to me, or maybe I'm just believing something I read on the internet… But it was like my sight, my smell, and my taste buds were all coming through full force like never before. I felt awake and alive like I never had before.

In the beginning, I was so optimistic about how easy quitting drinking would be. I was lost, I was naive, and I had no idea what was about to happen in my life. Let's jump back to the sober guy I had met right before all of this had gone down. Funny how God sends certain people exactly when you need them, huh? It was a huge wake up call to hear a recovering addict say to me "I can't be around someone like you" after I told him what had happened. He wanted nothing to do with me because he knew it would threaten his recovery. I got angry, and I felt like a piece of shit... but could you blame him? This really put things into perspective to me. I had been judging him for being an ex-addict, while I was partying myself into the Emergency Room. He was an EX-addict, and I was an ACTUAL addict.

I posted on Facebook that I was purging my life of alcohol, because that's what your normal, lost, confused 26-year-old trying to convince everyone that they are okay does, right? It was flooded with likes and comments, which was temporarily and abstractly encouraging. The truth is it didn't matter how many clicks I got on social media or how much I was supported in the beginning. I was about to embark on a journey that would change me forever, and I had no idea what was coming my way. It was going to be the most difficult 365 days of my life and it was going to change everything forever.

As far as support, I didn't think I needed any at this point. I knew what a strong, driven young woman I was and I felt I would be able to do this on my own, cold turkey. Since I was not the type of alcoholic that needed a drink to function everyday, I didn't feel many actual physical withdrawal symptoms at all. I hadn't needed alcohol daily to function before, so I wasn't feeling these types of physical needs. I just felt alive, so I foolishly thought it was going to be a piece of cake to stay sober. Though it was suggested to me multiple times, I never attended regular Alcoholics Anonymous meetings. The idea of sitting in a room with a bunch of people talking openly about their issues with alcohol didn't sound like something I thought I would benefit from. My main reason for thinking this was because I hadn't fully accepted the idea that I had been living like an alcoholic. I still saw myself as a partier and a binge drinker but had never labeled myself as an actual "alcoholic", so I didn't think that that made me like the people that attended AA meetings regularly.

If you follow my social media pages, I made a video on my YouTube channel when I had reached my first 30 days sober. I titled it "My Sober Story: Why I Quit Drinking" and it was the first time I had really opened up about the topic in a public way at all. When I watch the video now I look at myself and I just want to put my arms around that girl and protect her. I rambled on and on in an extremely optimistic way about how I was going to quit drinking. In my mind I was going to continue being the outgoing, fun-loving, bubbly girl I had always been. I intended on continuing to always have the perfect outfit on, the perfect winged eyeliner, and taking a ton of narcissistic selfies with all my girlfriends every weekend out partying and looking amazing. I loved being head strong and proving people wrong, so being able to continue my lifestyle without drinking was a challenge that I whole heartedly accepted and almost looked forward to. I wanted to do this and to prove to everyone that I could do it, and that I could do it my own way.

At this point, everyone joked about my always being the "DD" (designated driver) and thought it was awesome that I was still going out with my friends sober. Being the stubborn girl I was, I forced myself to be around alcohol still to prove to myself that I could continue to be the life of the party without it. My weekend routine would consist of still picking out my perfect little outfit, dancing at the bar, and reassuring every guy that offered to buy me a drink that I was "really drinking water" when they looked at me confused. I almost enjoyed and got off on the shock on their faces when I told them I was sober. I loved the idea that I was challenging the norm people had about individuals that had issues with drinking. I always loved paving my own path and breaking stereotypes, so this was just another opportunity for me to show the world I wasn't just your ordinary girl next door.

People thought it was badass that I could still have an eventful social life while I started my journey in sobriety. But what they didn't know was what happened every time I drove home at 2 am after I dropped off all of my drunk friends… My heart began to race, and I would start breathing really heavy. I would take deep breathes and drive myself home as the tears began to roll down my face. I had no idea who I was anymore without alcohol.

I was so uncomfortable in my own skin and in my own life. I would drive myself home in a full blown anxiety attack after a night of sober partying, trying to pull it together. I had been this person for so long and I was at the crossroads of trying to manage my old life and my new journey. I was literally struggling my way through an internal tug of war between the drunk party girl of my past and the young adult trying to make sense of everything and move on. This was an extremely rough time for me to navigate because I was having such a hard time letting go of who I thought I was. I loved being the life of the party, the girl everyone was looking at, the one posting photos every weekend of my fun-filled life. This was me. This was what I had been for so long. Was I ready to let that go?

I was clinging to my past like a naive little girl in an emotionally abusive relationship that everyone tells her to walk away from, but she just can't do it even though she knows better. I knew it was bad for me and that we would never be good together deep down in my heart. I knew that I could never be in a relationship with alcohol again like I had been in the past. If I tried to go down that road again I would just be playing with fire and it would only be a matter of time until I was right back to my old ways. I still don't think I was ready to cut the cord with my old lifestyle 100% just yet. I simply wasn't ready for it, and it was going to take me time to get there. So for months I stumbled through the motions of what my life had always been, just without the alcohol in it.

Many people still continued to suggest that I try Alcoholics Anonymous in the beginning of my sobriety. I looked into a couple locations and times, but something about the group setting aspect made me never want to actually go try it out. It was uncomfortable to me when I tried to picture what it would be like in my head. I didn't want to share my story with a bunch of strangers, because I was still so uncomfortable about it. I know that AA has thousands of success stories and works wonders for many, many people, but it was just not something that appealed to me. Maybe if I had caved and at least tried it out, it would have offered me a lot of support and help earlier on, but that never happened. I think another reason I never went was because I was still struggling to classify myself into a category of what I thought my relationship with alcohol was. I was not the person waking up and needing a drink to start the day. I had gone for periods of time without drinking before, so it was hard for me to actually call myself an "alcoholic" and completely believe it.

A few months into being sober I really got into dating apps. This totally doesn't surprise me anymore now that I have fully accepted the codependent ways of my past. I was being extremely reliant on the idea that I needed someone else in my life. Maybe if I had someone that loved me I would start to feel like myself again. Perhaps a relationship would be able to fill up the parts of me that I felt were so empty now. I wasted so much time on Tinder and Bumble shallowly swiping through men based on their physical appearance, and the men I was meeting were not always the best guys. I was so fixated on the idea of needing someone to be with me to be happy that I had no problem spending all of my time trying to find it.

I was looking for people and things to help me feel whole and complete when I was feeling so lost and confused. I had lost a huge part of my identity when I cut alcohol out of my life. When you are used to being a certain person that lives a certain way for so long, taking out the thing that made me who I had grown to know felt like I was taking away a part of myself. There was a huge gaping hole deep down inside of me, and I was trying to fill it with people and things to make myself feel complete again. I wasn't only trying to fill it, I was determined to fill it any way I possibly could.

I had said many times in the first few months that I wanted to go to therapy. I'm not sure if I was saying it because I believed what I was saying, or if I was just saying it because I knew it was what people around me wanted to hear. I was still so hesitant to admit that I needed help at this point that I did not start looking into finding a therapist at all. Although I thought I was diving head first into my issues with alcohol, I had barely even brushed the surface of them on my own. This naivety continued on for quite some time. I remember saying multiple times that I should go to therapy, but time after time I never actually fully believed what I was saying. I continued pushing forward without any type of support or help, and it surprises me now looking back that shit didn't hit the fan sooner than it did in my sobriety. I was just continually finding ways to distract myself from the reality that I wasn't dealing with the underlying issues, that my relationships, my career, and my life that had been the reasons for my binge drinking.

I got into a relationship early on in my sobriety, which I firmly believe was for the purpose of breaking the cycle. I was desperate for someone to just be there. I was struggling to get through the emotional rollercoaster that was becoming my life, and I needed something constant. He kept me from wanting to go out, and gave me a somewhat normal lifestyle for a while. I would spend my weekend evenings with him and it became a sort of routine spending time with my boyfriend and his family.

Having someone to spend time doing things with made me start to lose interest in going out more and more as time passed. I no longer felt the need to dress up and go out to the bars to dance with my friends anymore. I think part of the reason I enjoyed still going out so much was because I had been single and always hoping I'd meet the man of my dreams while I was out. The fact that I thought I would meet him throwing back shots at the bar is humorous to me now, but at the time it seemed appropriate because it was all I knew. I now realize that there is nothing attractive to a man about a girl so shit-faced that she doesn't even realize whats going on… except for the fact that he could probably take her home with him pretty easily if that's what he was looking for. No wonder I never met many men of substance or quality while I was stuck in my binge drinking days, right?

Things were better for a while in that relationship, and I was starting to realize that I could still have fun without being at a crowded bar watching everyone slam shot after shot. I dove 200% into this relationship because it was comforting to me in a time of chaos in my own head. My codependent ways were at an all time high, and I wanted to be with him constantly. It definitely wasn't the most ideal situation, and there was a ton of baggage and drama that came along with it. At the time I didn't really care because at least I had someone with me. As long as I had someone I was in a relationship with I thought that things would be fine. Surprisingly, I was able to navigate this relationship without much stress for most of the time we were together. But of course things eventually didn't go so smoothly, and things became less and less easy. The baggage and chaos that came along with this relationship were the last thing I needed while I was still in such a state of recovery emotionally and mentally. But nonetheless, it lasted for a while and was one of the more serious relationships in my young adult years. It kept me busy and kept my mind occupied and away from the thought of alcohol.

When I was nearing six months sober, things unexpectedly began to wear on me emotionally more than I ever imagined they would. I thought that I was halfway through my first year sober, and that if it was this easy so far that I would surely have no problem going forward. But this was when everything started to change, and it was completely out of my own control.

Around this point, the nightmares began. I would have such vivid dreams about being drunk, that I would wake up literally feeling like I had the spins and run to the bathroom thinking I was about to throw up. I would drink in a dream and feel such intense feelings of guilt and regret that I would wake up feeling absolutely horrible about myself. Of course, it was always a huge wave of relief to wake up and realize it was all just a dream, but the emotional impact of being back in that mind frame would carry over into my day and leave me feeling stressed and anxious. I was having dreams constantly that people were trying to help me stand up and walk when I was too drunk to even take one step on my own. I dreamt that I was driving a car drunk and getting into horrible car accidents. I would even dream that someone would find me with an empty bottle and I would try to convince them over and over again that I hadn't drank it. They would just keep telling me in the dream that I drank the whole thing myself and just didn't remember doing it. I would cry in these dreams and try to convince them that I "wouldn't do something like that after going this long" when they repeatedly convinced me that I had. The underlying issues I still hadn't began to deal with were starting to come through on their own, demanding to be heard through my dreams.

Things started to affect me emotionally without warning more often. I would get in bed and cry for absolutely no reason at the drop of a hat. I can remember a time my ex-boyfriend had been flipping through the channels to find something to watch on TV and I was so overcome with feelings of being depressed that I didn't even want to be near him. I walked to my bedroom and got into my bed, and of course he followed me. He asked if I was okay and all I managed to get out was a "no" before breaking down and hysterically crying for no reason at all. He held me while I cried for a long time. He asked what was wrong and I said I didn't know. I really didn't know why I was getting these intense rushes of emotions I had never felt before.

There wasn't ever any specific reason or trigger for these breakdowns I would experience at all. A lot of emotions and issues were coming to the surface in ways that were entirely new and unfamiliar to me. I was finally realizing that there were things I had never dealt with tucked away and hidden deep inside of me. I had been drowning them away with drugs and alcohol for so many years that I didn't even know how to process them now. Feeling so many new emotions at one time sent paralyzing waves of overwhelming anxiety over me constantly.

I needed help and it was starting to become clear to me that I couldn't do this alone. As much as I liked to think that I could take on anything life threw my way, it was a real splash of cold water to realize that I was wrong about that this time. I had been trying to just push down and ignore all of the issues and emotions that I would have normally just drank away. If you watch the YouTube video I made when I was six months sober, you can tell how uneasy and anxious I was during this time even talking about it. I was beginning to let all of the emotions and issues of my past start to surface, and it made me extremely uncomfortable doing so. Breaking down the walls of a dam holding back rushing waters is the only way I can try to describe to you how I felt at this time in my life. Every little thing felt like it was getting added to the top of a humungous pile of emotional baggage that was growing higher by the minute. The water that broke through the dam was crashing into me, and I was struggling to keep my head above the surface.

I suggested to my boyfriend that I wanted to find a new church, and I had one in mind that a few people had told me about in the past. I thought that maybe turning to Religion would offer me some sort of redemption and peace. He began attending church with me every week, and I found this new weekly habit extremely comforting.

It gave me a routine, a habit, and a place where I felt welcome. Going to church every week made me feel good, and I felt that I had found something positive to take up a portion of my weekends and get my mind in a better place. Things seemed to be leveling out again and I felt for a short time like my life was starting to become somewhat stable. I was a fool and once again being naive about the reality of things, I didn't realize that I wasn't anywhere near stable.

And then my boyfriend blindsided me, broke my heart, and left me. I was so incredibly numb. Alcohol had been the remedy for all of the emotions I hadn't wanted to feel in the past, and I didn't have the bottle to lean on this time. I remember the night he broke up with me, my mom came over to spend the night with me because she knew I was absolutely crushed. I laid awake in bed for hours… the entire night. I couldn't sleep. I couldn't eat. I couldn't turn off my mind. Hours and hours went by that night and all I did was lie in my full-sized bed next to my mom in a total daze. I don't think it had fully hit me yet that it was over.

Because I had become so codependent on being in a relationship early on in my sobriety, I really didn't know what I was going to do at this point without one. I had lost the one thing I had relied on so heavily in the beginning of my sobriety and I had nothing on standby to take its place. How would I fill this humungous void in my heart now?

I was supposed to be going on a cruise to the Bahamas with him for my 27th birthday present just a few days after this had happened. Needless to say, we were no longer going on the cruise. I realized that I had an entire week I had already taken off at work, and a half packed suitcase sitting on the floor in my bedroom. There were the new sunglasses we had gone shopping for and picked out together, mix and match pieces from several bikinis, and a new floppy sun hat that he had bought for me all lying on the floor next to the half empty suitcase. Looking at all of it, I panicked. I felt weak and helpless and since I didn't have alcohol or drugs to drown it out this time, I had to run from it because I wasn't quite ready to actually deal with it yet. I told my mom that I had to go somewhere. There was no way I was going to sit here all week thinking about the cruise I wasn't going on and the boyfriend that was gone. I couldn't be here and I wasn't ready to face this. So my mom, being the amazing woman she has always been, dropped everything, took the time off work, and said "Let's go to Vegas."

We spent several days exploring Vegas and the surrounding areas together. We ate delicious food, we talked a lot, and it helped me to get my mind off of things. We went to Zion National Park in Utah on one of the days of our trip. This was the first time I had really been in the mountains, and I fell in love with it. The natural beauty of the earth was so overwhelming to me, and something I hadn't seen much of as a young girl unless we passed it while driving down to Disney World. We spent a whole day hiking around and seeing all that Mother Nature had created. This day really showed me my love of travel for the first time. I was so happy just being in a new place and seeing new things. This trip would ultimately spawn my love of traveling that I still have today.

After getting back home from the trip, I was forced to face the music about what had really happened. In reality, I had no intentions of actually dealing with my feelings and emotions because I had never had to do that before. This was such a foreign idea to me that I slipped back into my old mindset of how to not deal with things like this in my life. I was uncomfortable with the idea of feeling vulnerable and hurt, so I went back to doing what I would always do.

Instead of drinking, I would just go out and party with my friends sober to take my mind off of things. I went out in my cute little outfit to the bar with my girlfriends the day after we got back from Vegas. I saw a hot guy working there as a bouncer and decided that that was what would make me feel better. This is exactly what I had always done… Rather than feeling the pain and working through the emotions, I would find someone else to want me to prove to myself that I was still in control and desirable by others. If I still had someone that wanted me then surely I hadn't completely lost all control yet.

I shoveled the emotional baggage I hadn't dealt with into a new rebound relationship, which ultimately ending up leading to the lowest point I'd ever hit. We were both on extreme rebounds, and spent an unhealthy amount of time together. He was at a bad place in his life, and so was I. Somewhere along the way we decided that we actually wanted to try to be together. This was a terrible idea. As a guy I know has said to me, "Sarah! You NEVER date the rebound!" Now I'm not saying that a rebound can never become something more, but this one was the biggest case of red flags, sirens flashing, and figurative 'do not enter' signs right in front of my very own eyes that there ever could be in life. Deep down, I knew that this probably wasn't a good idea. I simply did not care and kept moving forward with it because I just wanted someone else there to fill the empty spot, and I didn't care about the consequences. Someone wanted me and that was all that mattered at this point.

He cheated on me multiple times, manipulated me into giving him another chance, and was emotionally abusive to say the least. I had always been the strong, take-no-shit girl when it came to dating, but this time I was allowing someone to break me down to nothing and walk all over me. I had gotten to a new low point in life, where I questioned everything about myself. I was looking for other people to give me the answers. I was trying to make this man fill the empty parts of my heart and my soul, and he was never going to be able to do that.

I let this relationship drag along for SO LONG. I let him treat me like dirt. I caught him in so many lies that I barely even knew how to tell what the truth was anymore. After he cheated and I gave him another shot, there was a solid two weeks where things actually changed. I met his family and he even changed things about his physical appearance to prove to me that he was not the man he had been before. I was being a stupid little girl that was so hurt and desperate for love that I believed him. I ate up every word he said with a spoon. For the first time I felt like he actually genuinely cared.

How messed up is it that after he cheated on me I started to feel like he cared for the first time? Narcissistic manipulators are so talented at doing this that it is downright scary. Weak, lost little girls are the perfect prey for this type of scenario because we have no sense of self-worth.

Once I realized I had to get out, all of the emotions I hadn't been dealing with rushed in and hit me right in the face. It was like a light switch had been turned on inside of my head and I finally realized that the strong young woman I was still lived inside of me somewhere. She hadn't left, she had simply just gone into hiding for a while until it was her time to come to the front of the stage again. I couldn't believe I had been so blinded by what I thought was love, and that I had let myself be put down so low. Had I lost my damn mind!? What the hell was I doing!? Typically, this was when alcohol would come into play, when I felt like someone had threatened my pride or tried to hurt me, but this time I told myself no. I had come this far and reached nine months of sobriety. I wasn't going to let a few idiots ruin everything that I had accomplished so far.

I found myself extremely uncomfortable with the act of sitting at home watching a movie by myself on a weekend night, so I'd mindlessly swipe through Tinder instead to find someone else to fill the empty parts of my life. Although I had been able to identify that the situation I had been in was not healthy, I was still kind of stuck following my old ways. I was still talking to guys online and setting up dates and I didn't see anything wrong with it.

I actually ended up connecting with a guy from over the border in Windsor, Ontario in Canada that happened to be early on in his sobriety as well on one of these apps. We met up once to talk about our journeys so far being sober. It never went anywhere as far as a relationship goes, but we still text or message each other periodically just to check in on each other and see how we are doing. We congratulate each other on our milestones and have remained friends over social media. I connected with another guy around this time that was in recovery as well, and we immediately clicked. This also never progressed into anything romantic, but we too keep in touch about how we are doing every once in a while. This was the first time I felt some sort of support system in others that were sober too, and I wish I would have realized sooner what a positive and healthy thing it could be while living sober.

So there I was attempting to stand on my own two feet without a relationship for the first time in a long time, and the emotions were coming in full force again. I still didn't know how to deal with this mess of emotions I'd never allowed to surface before. I withdrew from my family, my friends, and everyone else. I no longer felt the desire to try to bring others into my life to make myself feel better at this point. I had never felt actual, full-blown depression, but I knew that what I was feeling wasn't a good thing. I would get home and look at the clock reading 4pm and wish it was later so I could just go to sleep. I felt tired and had little to no motivation for days on end. Anyone that knows me knows that I am the most optimistic, go-getter of a girl you could ever meet... so feeling this way really started to scare me. I knew something big was going on inside of me and that it wasn't good.

I knew now at just under a year sober that I had to get help. I had never felt these types of lows and I wouldn't be able to pull myself out of them on my own. This was when I returned to my faith again in a more serious manner. Church became my safe place, and my first form of therapy. I had dreams that were so vividly representing what I was going through directly related to biblical references that when I told a pastor about them he sat back in his chair and just said, "Wow." If you do not believe in God, a higher power, or any form of religion, this part might not make sense or have relevance to you, but I began to talk to God more and he sent me signs when I needed them most. Church was a huge help in my journey at this point, but I knew I still needed some sort of formal therapy with a professional.

5 | PICKING UP THE PIECES

This was where the healing began. I had been crushed to rock bottom and was just starting to pick up the pieces to rebuild them in a way that would make me stronger than ever before. I realized at this point that I could have never started to rebuild myself until I had been smashed to bits both emotionally and mentally. I literally had to fall apart and be broken into pieces to be able to pick them back up and turn them into something new. The physical act of quitting drinking had been the least of the hard work so far, and it was probably the easiest part of my transformation at this point. I was starting to realize that there was a lot more that I had to deal with and work through than just the alcohol itself... It was the underlying issues I had drowned in alcohol for years that I needed to face.

As my love for church grew stronger, I was going alone every weekend and actually looking forward to it. It was a little uncomfortable at first because I had been so used to going with both of my recent ex boyfriends. When I first thought back about both of them attending church with me, I was extremely spiteful and bitter about it. How dare they come to a place so holy and full of hope, MY safe place, on a foundation of lies? This was my new beginning, my journey to find faith in my sobriety and they sat in the seat next to me every week holding my hand when none of it was real. I was nowhere near ready to forgive and forget the pain they had both caused me yet. I was still clinging to it with quite the chip on my shoulder. It still boggles my mind sometimes that someone could cheat on me and then stand next to me in worship holding my hand before God every Sunday and not feel one tiny shred of guilt about doing so. But that is a whole other topic that I will never fully understand. Over time I was able to acknowledge that this journey in my faith was my own and nobody else's, and I continued attending on my own every weekend with my head held a little higher.

I spent a lot of time focusing on myself again even though it was uncomfortable for me at first. I wasn't used to being just myself without anyone else or anything else feeling like it completed me. I had to start finding things that made me feel whole again, but they had to be positive things this time around. I had to include these things in my life in a healthy way and not lean on them as a crutch in times when I lacked the backbone to stand on my own. For so long when I felt weak I had leaned on outside forces to give me the strength that I lacked inside. The first thing I had to work on was stopping this act of leaning on other things, because it was a terrible habit. It was time to find the strength inside of myself.

Finally, I began to fully accept the idea that maybe I should look into finding an actual therapist. I still can't believe that I didn't find a therapist until so close to my one year sober anniversary. I had thrown around the idea of it for the entire length of my sobriety, but as is the case with a lot of things in life you can lead a horse to water but you cannot make them drink it. You can't make someone get help until they actually want it. I realized now that not only did I want it… but that I needed it. I had stumbled through the first ten months of my sobriety and successfully not had a drop of alcohol along the way, but now it was time to actually start healing and fixing things. It was time to get into the heavy shit. I tried meeting with a pastor at the church I was attending, but it didn't go exactly as I'd hoped it would. Nothing at all against my church because I still attend weekly and I absolutely love it there, but it just wasn't the type of therapy I think I would benefit the most from. I began looking into multiple places to go, and settled on a female therapist in an office not too far from where I lived based on what she specialized in.

I'll never forget my first day of therapy. I knew it was going to be a rollercoaster, and I knew that I was going to be a hot mess having to relive and tell her everything about my past. I didn't wear much makeup that day because I knew it was going to be an absolute waterworks scene with my having to say everything out loud again. My mom went with me to the office because she knew how hard it was going to be for me, and she waited in the waiting room while I went in for my first appointment... Once again, this is a shining example of her undying love for me and how she always wanted to protect her little girl above all else. I was taking a huge step forward in my sober journey and I couldn't have felt more supported having her there by my side for it.

That first appointment I was an absolute mess. I literally sobbed through the entire hour of telling her all about my childhood, growing up, my downward spiral, losing control, and being the depressed mess I now was. I went through a pile of tissues that I am, oh, so grateful she had sitting on the table next to me. I talked a lot about my teenage years and my family. I talked about how many times I had been hurt by people I loved that I thought loved me back. I told her about every time my drunkenness had gotten me into some kind of trouble. I let every little thing flow out like word vomit.

It was strangely comforting and felt like a million pounds had come off of my shoulders. I realized that things from my past affected me emotionally a lot more than I ever thought they did when I began to tell her about them and lost all control, breaking down into tears over and over. I shared with her the time I had something put in my drink and couldn't get away from the guy on the couch at the party in Flint, and I let myself process for the first time in her office that something terrible had happened to me on that night. It was mind boggling to me that this was the first time I had fully processed and realized the extent of what had happened to me. It was like I was letting myself remember and accept a dark memory for the first time ever almost ten years later. How had I blocked it out for so long and just realized what had happened now?

About a year into my sobriety I uncovered something in therapy that I barely could piece together, but I knew deep down that something terrible had happened again. I had been partying in Windsor with my friends before I had turned 21 years old because that's what we always did before we were legal to drink in the U.S. One particular night I remember nothing past our pregaming and heading to the bar, but the night took a turn at some point. For some reason, something had happened that I had called my mother very upset and drunkenly pleaded with her to come pick me up in Canada while I was blacked out. She loaded into the car around 2 am with my older brother to come get me. I remember getting back to our shitty, run down hotel room at the Days Inn where my friends and I had been staying to get my stuff before my Mom got over the border and everyone kept asking me what was wrong. They could tell I was visibly upset and they kept asking me why I had dirt all over the back of my clothes. I had no idea why the back of my clothes were covered in dirt or why I had wandered back to our hotel alone after 2 am.

Where had I gone, and who had I gone with? How did the back of my clothes get covered in dirt and mud? Why was I so upset that I called my mother to drive over the border to come pick me up when I had planned on crashing at the hotel with my friends like usual? I doubt I will ever be able to fully remember anything about what actually happened that night, and the possibilities of what could have happened when I try to remember make me so uncomfortable that I'd rather leave it as a mystery to myself.

If I can stress anything about therapy, it would be that EVERYONE should go. Whether it was prompted by a major life event or not, I grew to love therapy and look forward to my weekly appointment. Letting go of everything and talking openly and comfortably about your deepest and darkest thoughts and feelings without judgment is extremely therapeutic. Some of the things I talk to my therapist about, I would never tell my friends or my family, but having an outsider that will listen without judgement gives you the opportunity to let out the things you may have been holding in. Letting go of your deepest thoughts and feelings can take away so much of the anxiousness and stress about things you have been harboring inside of yourself.

I began to realize that I loved the way I felt safe yet vulnerable in her office. I realized more about myself during my first year in therapy than I did in any of the 28 years I have been alive so far. So the bottom line I will stress is that therapy was life changing for me and I would encourage anyone to try it. Do not ever feel ashamed or embarrassed to go and to seek help if you need it. Working on yourself is an investment that will bring you more richness in return than you could ever imagine.

I knew initially that therapy was going to be hard for me because I hated admitting that I was weak or that I had failed at something. It made me feel less like the strong, independent woman that I had always prided myself in being by doing this. I had always been such a strong person, and always thought I could do anything I aimed to do on my own. Letting someone know all of the things about myself that I considered to be "flaws" and being so vulnerable was extremely out of my comfort zone, but I started to truly love the feeling of it over time.

While I hated identifying the things I thought were "wrong" with me, being able to say them out loud made me realize that some of them were just plain ridiculous. My ego had created these ideas of what or who I thought I had to be in the past to be accepted, and what I considered to be important in being "happy." I thought I had to have the most exciting lifestyle that would make others envious of me to be happy. I thought I had to have everything going perfectly in my life to be complete. I thought my life had to be like a highlight reel of someone's timeline on Facebook to feel like I was on the right path.

I had already began understanding more about my relationship with alcohol in the past, and more about myself in doing so. I realized that I consistently worked myself silly because I held onto the success in that area of my life when other areas of it weren't going as well. I realized that I spent an unhealthy amount of time with the guys I dated because I absolutely hated being alone. I realized that it was almost impossible for me to sit and watch an entire movie at home by myself without working on my laptop at the same time. I realized that I numbed emotions with alcohol rather than dealing with them over and over and over. I discovered numerous things about myself through therapy that I would have never acknowledged otherwise.

I hated not being busy, I hated spending time at my own place alone, and I hated not getting some form of reassuring attention from others at all times… Maybe that's why I even started writing this book. Maybe I still need others to give me the reassurance that I've always craved in life. But all of the things I have learned about myself have allowed me to break myself open and to be an open book for the first time in my life. It has taught me to not hide or tuck away the things about myself I consider to be flaws, because they are what makes me who I am.

This had been the most stable I had felt in my sobriety so far, and I was doing it one hundred percent alone. Nobody had gotten me to this point but myself, and I was responsible for all of the positive changes I was making in my life for the first time in a long time. Things started to feel calm. I was starting to accept myself and my past more than I ever had before. I fully grasped the idea that my troublesome past had built me into who I was today, and that it had given me the chance to rediscover myself as an even stronger person than I was before. The wheels really started turning in my head and things got so much easier with every day that passed.

I shared all of my milestone dates during my first year sober in YouTube videos and a lot of people were starting to comment and reach out to me through emails and comments daily. I realized the sense of community there was in the world of people living sober lives, and I still felt a little bit of that drive to be doing something more with what I had learned so far. It was so cool seeing how other people out there were relating to what I had been through.

I had gone back and forth with the idea of how long I would be sober for many, many times during my first year. I also threw around the idea of when I would drink again if I did. I had told myself I would go for a year, but then what? What would happen after a year? Did I really need alcohol back in my life at all? These questions were ones that I went over often. I didn't know yet how I would continue after I hit the one year mark, and the one year mark had grown to be something I started to carry a small amount of fear about. Would I be a failure if I tried to drink in a "healthy" or "normal" way after it passed? Would I live the rest of my life without it completely? I had no definite answer to these questions yet, so I figured I'd just ride out the first year and see where it took me. Part of me did still miss all of the fun I used to have going out with my friends. Although I knew it wasn't healthy for me to do those things again, I'd be lying if I said that a part of me didn't entertain the thought that maybe one day I would be okay to drink again. This dialogue was one I went over in my mind numerous times, and I never made a definite decision about what I planned to do after the one year mark during those first 365 days.

The last few months of my first year sober had been so empowering and inspiring. I had kicked alcohol for almost 365 days. If you had told me that a year before, I would have laughed at the idea of it. Never in a million years would I have thought that this was the path I would be going down. Throughout this year I was able to start discovering who I really was in my friendships, my family, my career, and in my relationships. I started to feel a deeper purpose for my being on this earth. I survived something I shouldn't have, and I felt the urge to do something about it. I had started to believe that I was saved because I was meant to share my story with people (hence the YouTube videos and the creation of soberAF.com). I finally was more comfortable in my own skin than I had ever been before, and I was ready to start opening myself up to the world in hopes that someone somewhere would benefit from what I had to share.

I was attending therapy weekly and growing stronger emotionally and mentally with every day that passed. I was starting to acknowledge my self-destructive habits and patterns of my past, and realized that I had been leading myself back into the same situations over and over again for years. Being able to accept my own part in being responsible for these destructive cycles in my life took a long time for me to do. Being as stubborn as I was, I did not want to admit that I had actually played a major part in the self-destructive ways of my past.

When you have no other option but to accept the fact that you were just as responsible for your actions as any outside factor you had tried to blame it on, you eventually will be forced to see it in a truthful light. Being able to accept this idea and move past it just showed me that if I could almost ruin my life with my own ways, then surely I could be the biggest force in turning all of those ways around too. My new focus would be to play an active part in creating my best life... the happiest, most positive, fulfilling life I could possibly create for myself.

I didn't need the alcohol-fueled attention I used to receive from guys at a bar anymore. Now I could go on a date and have an actual conversation with someone who was genuinely interested in who I was and what I was doing in my life. I no longer needed to go out partying to spend time with friends. Now I could have a girls night in, meet for dinner, or go see a movie with people who showed that they were still around when the party wasn't. I lost quite a few friendships along the way when I changed my life, but the ones I have now carry so much more meaning than any of the ones I used to take shots with every weekend. I no longer tried to make plans any time I had a day off or an evening free. Now I could enjoy cooking myself a nice dinner and binge watching Netflix on a weekend night and enjoy it. I was beginning to see myself blossom into a whole new person living a whole new life.

The thought of the future had become so hopeful and exciting to me once I was able to look at things from this new place. I daydreamed about the potential of what I could achieve in my life now that my mind and my body were so much clearer without alcohol constantly flooding them. I wanted to be successful in my career and feel proud of my accomplishments. I wanted to cherish amazing friendships with the people that were a part of my life. I wanted to grow closer to my family and repair what I had almost destroyed.

The sky seemed like the limit for me now, and I had gained an unwavering hope for all of the things that were ahead of me that I couldn't even see yet. As my one year sober date drew closer and closer, I still harbored a sort of fear for that actual day. Even though I had come so far already and felt like I had grown so much, that date still lurked in the back of my mind and carried a lot of fear with it.

6 | DAY 365

The night before my one year sober date, I was alone. I had said multiple times that I wanted someone to be with me on that day. I had also said that I wanted to leave and go on a trip so that I wouldn't be here when that day came. The thought of being far, far away on a beach seemed like a much better idea in my mind. I didn't want to accept the fact that being somewhere far, far away and beautiful would not change the fact that the calendar was still going to be on that date on May 25th 2016. That day was going to come no matter where I was or who I was with. I thought that maybe if I had someone with me on that day it wouldn't be as hard for me to handle emotionally. If a guy I was dating was there and really cared about me, maybe it would make it all feel better. I was absolutely terrified of how emotional it would be for me to face that day without someone else. I went over numerous scenarios in my mind of how I would navigate my one year sober date, all of which involved being with someone or being somewhere else to take my mind off of things and not truly having to face what it meant. I was legitimately terrified of facing that day again when I should have been feeling excited, accomplished, and extremely proud of myself for such a huge accomplishment.

The night before my one year sober date at around the time I had been rushed to the emergency room 365 days prior, I dropped to my knees next to my bed and buried my face in my hands. I completely and totally lost it. I can't even describe to you exactly how I was feeling because it was a messy combination of feeling like a helpless child, and a small, small person in the big picture of the world. I realized how precious my life was, and I realized that I had almost selfishly given it up. I was so careless with my one life, while others that were actually sick or hurting were so desperately fighting for their own. It was one of the most emotional nights of my entire life. It hit me like a ton of bricks while I knelt next to my bed, my face buried in the sheets with my hands folded just above my head in prayer.

That moment was the most overwhelming feeling of gratefulness I have ever experienced in my life. I realized the full extent of what had happened for the first time. I realized that one year ago exactly my body had been shutting down on itself. I realized that I had been somehow saved, and I realized just how lucky I was. Through my sobbing I said out loud "I'm so sorry" and "Thank you." I felt the overwhelming need to be thanking whatever or whoever in the Universe pulled me through. I was thanking God, I was thanking whatever angels I might have had watching over me, I was thanking the Universe… I wasn't sure exactly who or what I was thanking but I just had the strongest feeling to be grateful and thank someone.

I tried to calm myself down by telling myself "You made it" and "You're fine-you did this." If I had ever felt or seen myself act crazy in my entire life, this scene in my bedroom surely would have been how I would picture it. I felt just like Angelina Jolie in the movie *Girl, Interrupted*, where she plays a girl living inside of a mental institute. I probably looked insane, like I was having a complete and total meltdown… because I was. Everything had come full circle finally and it was hitting me real heavy.

I broke down that night just as I had 365 days before. I cried because I was not in a hospital, but in the beautiful place I am fortunate enough to call my home. I cried because of the people who are no longer in my life, but so grateful for the people that came into it, or had stayed a part of it. I cried because of how I had hurt my family, but also because those relationships had been rebuilt. I cried because I had been so hurt by people I put my love into, but grateful for them for making me stronger. I cried because of the faith I had once lost, but in awe of the place my faith had now led me back to. I cried and I thanked God for saving me, for making me strong enough to get through this, for slamming on the brakes and giving me the opportunity to rewrite my life... and that's exactly what I was doing.

Crying on my knees, I let everything from the past year go. I let go of the fear that I wouldn't be able to stay sober. I let go of the fear of being alone. I let go of the fear that I would be missing out on things in life without alcohol. That night I realized I didn't need friends, a man, or anyone else there to finish those 365 days. I did it, and I did it on my own.

When I woke up on May 25th 2016, I felt a new sense of calmness. After my total meltdown from the night before, I felt like I had been able to release all of my anxiety and fear about hitting this date. What had I been so afraid of? I was alive, I was healthy, and I was living my life.

My one-year sober date conveniently fell on the day I go to therapy so we spent the entire appointment that morning talking about my meltdown the night before, how I felt on the big day, and reflecting on how much had changed in my life. We really focused on how much I had changed for the better and how much more positive my life had become. I felt proud and I felt accomplished. I had made it those 365 days through some of the darkest times of my life. I had faced my underlying issues and anxieties head on one right after the other. I had come to terms with the fact that I do live with depression and anxiety, as much as I had never wanted to believe it or acknowledge it in the past. I had accepted the fact that I did have an issue with alcohol, and it had almost cost me everything. I had accepted the fact that what happened was not a bad thing in the big picture of my life, but rather that it was a huge blessing.

Without that night in the hospital, I would have never gotten here. I was now able to look at what had happened as a positive thing in the long run. I would have never changed the way I had been living my life if it had not happened. This was a time in my life when I was whole heartedly believing the idea that "everything happens for a reason". I think some people just use that saying as a way to make sense of the bad things that happen and the hard times in their life. But this was the first time I truly and entirely believed it.

Without everything that happened in the previous 365 days, I would not have gotten to the good place I was in now. It gave me a way of giving what had happened a silver lining, and I think it mentally helped me accept it and use it to better myself. I had heard a quote at some point about how without darkness we would never know what light is, that the bad times make us appreciate the good times ever more. And it's an interesting concept and way of thinking… If we had no idea what darkness was, would we acknowledge light? Would the good things in life be identified as being "good" if we had no idea what a "bad" thing was? This way of thinking helped me to see everything I had gone through as leading me to something new and better for my life. Without the bad times, I would have never realized how much better things were now.

After my therapy appointment on my one year anniversary of my sober date, I walked into a tattoo shop and asked if they could take me as a walk in. I got the roman numerals for May 25th 2015 tattooed on my inner left arm. I didn't get a tattoo to be trendy or a badass, or to commemorate my sober date. I got this tattoo to remind myself of the first day of the rest of my life. Not the life I knew, but the new life I had embarked on. I say that this was the first day of the rest of my life because everything from that day forward was a step towards where I was supposed to be and who I was supposed to be all along.

May 25th 2016 was not as eventful or crazy as I had imagined it would be. I had scared myself so much about this date for so long, but once I reached it I realized that it was just another day in my life.

Of course it was a day worth recognizing my accomplishment of being sober for an entire year, but it also just felt like a normal day to me. I was just relieved that it had finally come, and that all the worries and fears I had attached to it for so long were nowhere to be found.

7 | WHAT DO I DO NOW?

Moving into this new territory and lifestyle was still extremely uncomfortable for months. I had no idea who I was or what I was doing in the beginning of my sobriety at all. I went into this new chapter of my life so desperately trying to cling to the ways of my past at first. I should have realized sooner that a lot of things in my life needed to change, but that didn't happen as quickly as I hoped it would have. My life had been the same twisted routine of dressing half naked, drinking as much alcohol as humanly (or inhumanly) possible, and meeting guys with my girlfriends... The location, the people, and the types of alcohol may have changed week to week, but the routine predominantly stayed exactly the same. If I was dating someone at the time, they either just got mixed into the routine or I fell out of the pattern for a while and things actually did change for a hot minute. Ultimately they would screw it up, or I would screw it up, and back to the routine I fell. Back to short dresses, high heels, and shot glasses.

Once I had my complete emotional breakdown after those two disastrous relationships and started therapy, I slowly came to the realization that I needed to start a new routine. The routine from my past was not healthy or productive, and it was doing nothing to help me along the way in my sobriety. Forcing myself to be in a bar while being sober is like forcing yourself to sit in a doughnut shop all day while you're on a diet… You can see the thing you're depriving yourself of, you can smell it, and you're surrounded by the thing you know you are trying to avoid.

Somehow I have incredible will power and never slipped up once along the way. I'm not sure many people would be able to do it, but somehow I was able to do it. In some twisted, weird way it was extremely satisfying to me that I had been able to maintain my lifestyle while just removing the alcohol from it. It was like a big middle finger in the air to everyone who thought I wouldn't be able to stay sober, but was it healthy or positive to my journey in any way? Probably not.

I discovered in therapy that I was extremely uncomfortable not being busy and being alone. I had always been the party girl, social butterfly type for all of my adult life so not going out with friends constantly made me feel like I was losing part of my identity. I was so accustomed to always going, going, going… Getting dinner and margaritas at this place after work, pregaming and getting ready downtown at a friend's apartment, going to this bar first, passing out at so and so's place… It was a never ending social whirlwind for days.

I never had a lot of free time and I was used to filling a day with things to do if I had a day off. Even if a day was filled with working from home, I had to fill it with something to keep myself busy. I never went places alone often in my young adult life either. It was an unfamiliar thing to me, so I always called a friend or even my mother to go run errands with me to fill the time and the space daily.

When I began acknowledging and facing my underlying issues for why I drank in therapy, this was one that I never realized I had along the way. It became very clear to me at first when my therapist asked me what I like to do for fun in my free time and I sat awkwardly in silence for a moment. I truly couldn't think of an answer. I knew I liked going out to eat, but that didn't seem like a valid answer to the question. I loved doing makeup, but that fell into the category of work since I do it for a living now. She pressed on about what my hobbies were, what I enjoyed doing in my free time, and what I enjoyed the most... I was struggling and grasping at straws to come up with some sort of an answer to give her. We quickly came to the conclusion that I wasn't giving myself time to do things that I enjoyed that weren't associated with work somehow.

On a typical day, I was waking up and doing emails or working on my laptop until I had to go to work at the cosmetic counter I worked at part time. Some days I would work out in the morning when I woke up and about once or twice a week I was getting ready for work early so that I could film a new YouTube video before leaving for the day. When I got home I would make dinner, clean up, do any work around the house, and then sit down to watch some TV shows with my laptop on my lap pretty much the entire time. I was usually busy responding to more emails, editing video footage, making Instagram posts, or writing blog posts in the evening.

On the weekends I worked with my business doing bridal makeup. We would get up early to work a wedding group, maybe grab some lunch together after, and then I would keep working from home the rest of the day or go visit one of my friends and go out to dinner. Do you see the pattern here yet? I filled all of my days with things to do. Most of the time they were not things I chose to do, but work I felt I had to do to keep myself busy. Seeing my friends to grab dinner once or twice a week was the only time I actually stopped working.

Having success in the entrepreneurial sector of my life always made me feel better because I still was successful in that area of my life. Really I think I was also just trying to keep myself busy so that I would not miss my old partying ways. If I kept myself busy and occupied then I didn't leave myself any time to sit around and process the feelings I so desperately tried to avoid for so long. But, of course, I learned in therapy that working through it and not avoiding it was the healthiest way to get through it, so we brainstormed how I could change this habit of mine. It was more difficult than I thought it would be.

I made a conscious effort to figure out what I could use to

replace the alcohol and the partying in my former lifestyle. I had tried to replace it with men and relationships, and that had been a real shitshow. Maybe if I had made better choices in the men I was dating it could have gone better, but I just wasn't there yet when it came to making good choices in dating. You will hear ALL about that in a later chapter. I had tried to replace partying by just working constantly, which was extremely productive, but I still wasn't giving myself the down time to just RELAX. I was simply keeping my mind occupied without fulfilling any of my inner needs.

I remember one particular evening telling myself I was going to sit down early with Kaya and cuddle up with a big blanket in my pajamas, make some popcorn, and watch a movie on a weekend night. I got all ready, curled up with my little pup, lit one of my candles, and found something on Netflix to watch. About fifteen minutes into the movie I found myself reaching for my phone out of habit. I mindlessly scrolled through Instagram photos for a few minutes and then opened my Bumble app to see if I had any new matches. When I realized what I was doing I stopped and put my phone down, but within minutes I began feeling stir crazy again. I couldn't even sit and watch the first half hour of a movie without doing something else at the same time. What the hell was wrong with me? I realized in that moment that what we talked about in therapy was absolutely true… I could not just turn my mind off and relax.

I always had this fear that without going out to party I would be missing out on something, and I didn't want to miss out on anything. I wanted to be at every fun event, be around a bunch of fun people, and live every day of my life to the fullest. I was guilty of being one of those girls that had to take five million selfies with her girlfriends all dolled up to go out and post them all over the internet for a bunch of likes and comments. I wanted people to always see that I was having fun and looked great, probably to cover up the fact that I was struggling so much underneath it all. I was worried that if I wasn't around that people would forget about me, that I wouldn't still get all of the attention I had grown to be so reliant on throughout my life.

What a warped sense of self-worth and desperate need for approval I had conjured up in my pretty little mid-twenties head, huh?

My therapist urged me to stop working by a certain time every night, "turn off", and do something for myself. I couldn't believe how almost impossible it was for me to actually try to do this. I started to feel like when I did spend time at home by myself that the feelings of being lonely would eventually seep in if I didn't preoccupy my thoughts with something to do. Being alone with myself and my thoughts would dim my mood within a very short amount of time. I would start to feel like I was in some sort of a funk or a bad mood that I couldn't snap out of. At that point, I would typically go to bed because I didn't want to deal with it. I didn't want to and I wasn't ready to deal with it yet, but at least I was starting to actually FEEL these things for the first time in my life. I didn't realize it at the time, but it was the first time I let myself start to actually feel my emotions in their entirety.

I first discovered that giving myself little things to look forward to daily seemed to keep my mood up and keep my mind off the fact that I was missing out on the party that still raged on without me there. I started to slowly miss those people, those places, and those alcohol-fueled nights less and less as time went by. I was shocked at how much giving myself the silliest, tiny little "me" things to look forward to started to make me hate being alone a little less day by day.

Some days I would find a recipe of something that sounded amazing for dinner and was somewhat healthy (okay, not always healthy… let's just be honest here). I would go to my local grocery store or farmers market to get the ingredients needed to make myself an amazing meal. I would turn up some music, get in my comfy clothes, and sing and dance around in the kitchen cooking it up for myself. I have always loved eating and have been blessed with a fairly good metabolism thus far in life, so food has always been something I have thoroughly enjoyed. Something about the act of preparing a delicious meal for myself and sitting down to enjoy it alone became a huge act of self-care for me. Doing this made me feel fulfilled, healthy, and it did more than just satisfy my physical hunger. It wasn't just filling my stomach, it was starting to fill my bruised and battered soul. This became quite a regular occurrence in my place, and I started to look forward to my cooking time at home. Kaya surely didn't mind all the amazing table scraps that somehow always seemed to make their way into her dog bowl either.

I started making plans for myself to see my friends more often. We were all growing older and our lives were starting to branch off into many different paths. The friends I maintained and grew closer with during my sobriety are the ones I will forever cherish the most, because during this time I discovered what true friendships look like.

Some of my friends were getting married and starting lives with their husbands, and others were becoming first-time moms. Not going out and partying meant finding new ways to spend time with friends, and at first I felt like I was constantly just asking everyone if they wanted to go get dinner. Dinner was the one way I already knew I could spend time with people without partying, because it was still a social thing in a social setting. I wasn't fully accepting the idea yet that you can actually spend time with people doing nothing when you have a deep and solid friendship, so there were many dinner invites on my end. I would try to solidify plans with friends at least twice a week, to give myself something social to look forward to and to keep my new (and old) friendships growing. Over time I eventually grasped the idea that you can just go to a friends' house and hang out and you don't always have to have something specifically planned out.

There was a time period when I was visiting friends at home with their newborn babies that I would become overwhelmed with sadness. This is what I had always dreamed of when I was a little girl… meeting the man of my dreams and having little babies of my own. I always saw myself starting a happy little family fairly young, but that hadn't happened for me. As I visited and held their beautiful little babies I would be trying to push back the thoughts of how much time I had wasted. I had been drowning myself with alcohol day after day while all of these people in my life were growing, maturing, and moving forward in theirs. I had been stuck in the partying phase when everyone else was already growing up and becoming adults.

Over time I was able to overcome this feeling, and take comfort in the idea that it just wasn't my time yet. I began to enjoy seeing my friends and spending time with their little ones so much. Now I will even host Sunday brunches at my place with the babies, where all of us bring a dish and baby proof my townhouse so that we can all catch up. We get to spend some time together, drink coffee, and watch the little ones play. It's crazy to think that my Sunday mornings went from being hungover on a stranger's couch to hosting brunches like I'm freaking Rachel Ray with babies crawling all over me.

Hosting get-togethers at my place became my way to still have my fun and have my social time with friends, but in a new and healthier way. Rather than hanging out at a bar wasted, I learned to absolutely love having people over. I hosted LulaRoe parties, Pure Romance parties, and I even hosted my own birthday party where I whipped up a "make your own nacho bar" complete with alcohol-free "mockaritas" with sliced limes and salt for the rims. I loved hosting my Sunday brunches and my weekend Girls Nights with endless amounts of pizza and yummy snacks. I had always been a social butterfly, and this was my new way of keeping that part of me alive. I loved having a full house and I loved sharing good times and good food with amazing people. Entertaining at my place was my healthy way of recreating the party scene in my new life. I was still able to hang out with my girlfriends, laugh until we cried, not be "alone", and do it all in the comfort of my own place in leggings... And we all know everything in life is much better in leggings.

Something that made it a lot easier for me to actually enjoy being at home so much now that I wasn't going out was making my place someplace I enjoyed being. I'd always had cute decorations in my place, but I decided to redecorate a lot after my sober life started. I wanted a place to call home that felt safe, comfortable, and just "like home". I wanted a place I could come back to that I enjoyed being in. I had been so uncomfortable with being home and being alone for so long, that making it a cozier, more appealing place for me helped me out a lot. I wanted to create my own little oasis or my "safe place" that I looked forward to spending time at.

I have always been a very visual person, and I like things to be very visually pleasing to the eye. Room by room, I began to take on small projects of redecorating. I had been saving so much money now that I wasn't going out constantly and buying new outfits all the time that I could actually afford to comfortably buy more expensive, nicer things for my place. I bought pieces of furniture, pieces of art for the walls, and changed all the color schemes in my home to be very white, bright, and incorporate a lot of neutrals. Everything looked a lot calmer and more peaceful this way, and I could just picture myself coming home to curl up with a blanket and my pup at the end of the day to wind down so easily now.

I had created a sanctuary for my mind, my body, and my soul. I noticed that I began spending a lot more time at home. The best part was that I was no longer dreading it or felt as uncomfortable being home alone. Sure, I still felt the loneliness seeping back in at the end of a Saturday night spent by myself sometimes, but I was growing stronger and stronger to overcome it with each day that passed. Now sometimes when I was out I caught myself looking forward to getting home, excited to be there and spend time in my newfound little oasis I had created for myself.

As I grew to absolutely love my place and being at home more often, I discovered a lot of things that I could give myself to look forward to during my nights in. Of course I had grown to love preparing meals for myself as I already went over, but over time I discovered more things I enjoyed at home. I really dove into Netflix, and discovered that I love a lot of indie movies and documentaries that I stumbled on while looking for things to watch. I loved documentaries about people that had overcome their struggles, and as you can imagine I loved watching people overcoming addictions, overcoming weight loss struggles, and accomplishing great things in general. I will admit there were a few series that I totally binge-watched entire seasons of in one day. Something about being a hermit in my place and binge watching my favorite shows became highly appealing to me, while I would have never imagined it would be. I watched numerous movies about love stories, life changes, and any other story plot you can imagine. Movie nights became my little nights in to relax, and with each movie I became more comfortable with putting down the phone and the laptop while I watched them.

There were many things I grew to enjoy in my new life, another one of them was focusing on my health. I had always been healthy in the fact that I remained around a normal weight for my height. I'm not sure how I managed this with the thousands of empty calories I consumed in alcohol on the weekends followed by a trip through the Taco Bell drive thru at 3 am on the regular. I guess I really did have a fantastic metabolism like I always joked.

In my quest to remain "perfect" and desirable to others I had always worked out somewhat regularly. During the week I ate pretty healthy to avoid gaining excess weight that would prevent me from looking as hot as I thought I should look in my skimpy outfits at the bar. The transformation I made physically after I stopped drinking was mind blowing, and it really put into perspective for me how powerful alcohol was over not only my mind and my actions, but also over my entire body. Within the first few months of being sober, I shed all of my "puffiness" weight I usually carried around from the alcohol.

I cooked healthier foods and became a lot more interested in the things I put into my body. I began to fuel my body with things that were good for it, which were much better than the drunk munchies I had inhaled every weekend in the past. Now don't get me wrong... if the girl wants pizza or a burger, she's gonna eat pizza or a burger, but learning about the things that were best for me and my body was very interesting to me. My body leaned out, my face looked thinner, and I couldn't believe it that even my early signs of wrinkles had softened on my skin. A friend at work even admitted to me the other day that she was looking through my older makeup photos on Instagram and noticed that I actually looked younger NOW, two years later. I had never grasped the idea of just how much alcohol could change my physical appearance. People I hadn't seen in a while would see me and say how different I looked, pointing out that I had lost weight, my skin looked healthy and glowing, and I just looked "different" to them.

Towards the end of my days with alcohol, I had began to struggle with very intense arthritis. Arthritis has always run in my family, and I was horrified that it was already affecting me in my mid-twenties. It traveled throughout my body over a very short amount of time. My right ankle and big toe would swell and I would limp through the beginning of my run when I would work out on the treadmill. The arthritis in my hip was so painful sometimes that I was popping Ibuprofen multiple times a day. I couldn't even sleep with a pillow anymore at night because my neck and shoulders were so stiff and aching that I would wake up feeling even worse than when I went to sleep.

I blamed it on my career in the beauty industry at the time, and I began to acknowledge that I would probably need carpel tunnel surgery within the next year because my right wrist wouldn't even bend to the point where I could do an actual push up anymore. If I held my wrists side by side it actually looked larger than the other wrist from the swelling. Lastly I developed Iritis in my right eye… which basically means the inflammation seen in arthritis had traveled into my eye. I didn't even know you could get arthritis in your eye, but when my vision blurred out and I was immediately sent to an eye specialist, I walked out with a diagnosis of Iritis and a prescription for steroid eye drops in hand. My body had turned into that of an 80-year-old woman by the age of 26.

I had gone to the doctor numerous times and had numerous tests done trying to figure out what was going on. The tests came back negative for early onset rheumatoid arthritis. My blood work rejected the idea that I possibly had Lupus or some other disease that could cause the inflammation. I did lots of blood work and X-rays, all with no real answers coming back other than that I had inflammation in my bloodstream. I went to a chiropractor for months, and the pain never got better. I did test after test at the doctors and never got any answers.

Fast forward to a month or so into my sobriety and one day I realized out of nowhere that the pain was gone. It was gone like it had never been there at all. My wrists were able to bend again, my ankles were able to run, I slept with big, comfy pillows again, and my eyesight was completely back to normal... Call me crazy but all of this happened to magically go away coincidentally when I stopped drinking? I highly doubt it. Upon researching it on my own and talking to my doctors about it, we had concluded that the high levels of alcohol I had been introducing into my bloodstream were probably causing the inflammation in my body. When I realized that alcohol had been HURTING me to that extent, it was crazy to wrap my head around it. I once again realized how powerful alcohol was when I thought about how it had reeked absolutely hell on my young adult body for so long.

Seeing how alcohol had been destroying my body before, I became so passionate about taking care of it now. In a way I felt like I was nursing myself back to health physically, after I had been so hard on my body for so long. I began going to bed a little earlier and getting a good night's sleep regularly. I began working out more and learned that I really enjoyed long runs with good music. I would completely zone out on these runs, and it became a great time to clear my mind and my thoughts. I began lifting weights and seeing my body grow stronger day by day was so empowering.

I had always been somewhat small, but now I could see the strength my body was capable of achieving. Seeing my body change into one that is strong, healthy, and taken care of has been amazing to see. Being able to both see and feel my transformation physically has made me feel so much more grateful and appreciative of my body.

I have always loved listening to music. Being in the alcohol and drug-fueled electronic music scene in Detroit clearly had brought around numerous negative factors into my young adult life. I know some people are able to enjoy the music and not get wasted or experiment with drugs while doing it, but I just wasn't one of those people. I had always loved the way I could dance to the beat without a care in the world. I could move my body and feel absolutely free while the bass pulsed loudly through every inch of my body, and feel goosebumps when a favorite song truly hit my heart. I loved everything about music... You could escape, you could be someone else, and you could let go of everything as it came over you. I still love electronic and house music to this day, and it is even playing softly in the background as I write with my cup of coffee this morning. The beats gave my body life and made my body move from the energy of the sounds.

After I got sober, I definitely started to explore other areas of music and discovered a surprising love for country. Trust me, I know, I never saw that one coming either! Something about the newer country music is just so playful and fun. Of course I'm also a sucker for a good, romantic love song too... I am a girl, remember. Music became a passion of mine and became a bigger part of my everyday life. I enjoyed listening to it constantly and discovering new artists and songs, and I started going to see shows every once in a while as well. The last show I went to was Rufus Du Sol in Detroit, and they were even more amazing live than I ever imagined possible. I've had the itching to even tattoo "innerbloom" somewhere on my body since I fell in love with the song live... and I love the idea of the word innerbloom, like a flower blooming in the deepest parts of our inner body and soul.

On days when my mood was in a total funk or I just felt a little blah, I began turning to self-help and motivational books and podcasts. I found myself so inspired and drawn to female authors and life coaches, and their passion and drive stirred things up inside of me each time I read or listened to their work. Anytime I needed to hear some words of motivation to raise my spirits or encouragement along the way, I knew this was becoming such a positive and healthy way to do so. My morale would be raised, my mood would be lifted, and I would feel like I could do anything I set my mind to after listening to their words.

I will admit that I am not one to sit down with an actual book in hand and read a lot of the time. Number one, I'm just a very active person and I think I would go stir crazy sitting down for that length of time. Number two, my schedule tends to get pretty full. I think it would take me a year to finish a book if I only read it when I was sitting around with nothing to do. Number three, to be absolutely honest with you... reading makes me fall asleep. Something about reading just makes my eyes get heavy and I will literally start to doze off and not even remember the last sentence I just read. My saving grace became audiobooks, and I began a continuous hot and heavy love affair with them.

If you haven't check out Audible, I HIGHLY recommend it. I listen to my audiobooks from my iPhone most of the time either linked up to a Bluetooth speaker while I'm cooking or cleaning at home, through my headphones while I run, or on my car radio while I'm driving. It literally is the most convenient thing in the world for me being able to listen to books anytime and anywhere. (Head over to audibletrial.com/sarahordo to get a free 30-day trial. I promise you that you will love it!)

My first true girl crush when it comes to female empowerment is Cara Alwill Leyba, the author of many books and poetry writings that I grew so much from in the beginning. Her book *Girl Code* was just one of those books that pulled at my heartstrings and really hit home for me. I related to her as a spiritual woman, as a dream chaser, and as a entrepreneur. Her poetry book *Stripped* became the equivalent of a personal thirty second therapy season on every page.

Not only is Cara a true inspiration to women everywhere to follow their heart and their passions, but she is truly one of the most humble, personable, and compassionate women I have ever encountered. We connected over Snapchat and email one day, and I couldn't believe that a best-selling author was so talkative and friendly with someone she barely knew. Her ability to connect with her readers and followers is something that makes her one of my favorite people to follow on social media. Every day, she shares incredible content and inspiration for women everywhere. Her podcasts on iTunes are the perfect little mood-boosting, girl power motivators. I often listen to them when I need a little morning pick me up. I can't thank Cara enough on behalf of all of us for always being our own personal cheerleader and motivator, leading her girl gang to do amazing things in this world.

When it came to becoming more connected to my spiritual side and the powers of the Universe, I really related to all of the works by Gabrielle Bernstein. *The Universe Has Your Back* really guided me and helped me to be open to all that the Universe and higher powers can show us in terms of guidance and love. Her book *Spirit Junkie* was so eerily on par with my story that it was almost like I was listening to my own biography at times. She too struggled with addiction, began her journey through sobriety after hitting rock bottom, and struggled to rebuild herself along the way. Her story hit so close to home that I couldn't help but feel connected to all of her work. I will admit I still struggle with the meditation aspect of her work. It is something new and quite foreign to me, but I have become more and more comfortable with embracing those calm, quiet, reflective moments over time.

I also really enjoyed a few books from Shauna Niequist, including *Bittersweet*. Shauna has such a soft yet raw account of the rough times in her life and shares every emotion along the way. I truly felt like I was walking with her each step of the way and feeling every emotion she described as if it was happening in my own body in her stories.

I had truly started to fill my time with things that made me feel alive and full of life. I started to feel like I wasn't missing out on much anymore in my sober journey. I began to feel so fulfilled by the things I did in my daily routine that I didn't even want to go to a bar or think about partying all night. Being at home or doing things that made me happy had become so much more appealing to me than the ways of my past. I never saw it coming, but I had begun to love the time I spent alone doing things for myself. Who would have thought that the social butterfly, party animal of the century would morph into this? I was now the homebody extraordinaire who was mastering the slow cooker and making the perfect baked chicken parmesan on a Saturday night. I would then cuddle up with Kaya to watch a chick flick while my favorite scented candle flickered on the antique gold tray I found to go perfectly on my living room ottoman. Talk about becoming the polar opposite of the girl I used to be...

8 | "WASTED" TIME

Any single girl nearing the end of her twenties can tell you, that during this time in her life there is an endless abundance of weddings, baby showers, engagements, and other sort of "adult" milestone markers you'll see happening to your friends. I can scroll through my Facebook news feed on any given day to see someone I went to high school with posting their first ultrasound photo or showing off their new engagement ring. My refrigerator is often decorated with RSVPs and baby shower invites that span the entire summer. I have watched some of my closest friends bring beautiful little humans into the world and say "I do" to their new husbands or wives. While I am so happy and excited for them and love being able to share in these huge moments with them, I'd be lying if I didn't say that at times I am so incredibly jealous of them that it has brought me to tears. I have left weddings early to drive around aimlessly to try to calm down and clear my head as the tears roll down my face.

Looking back, I'm not surprised that I am 28 years old and single, with no beautiful children of my own to raise yet. Why? Mostly because I was too busy passing out on someone's couch at 3 am or drunkenly telling off the latest guy I was kind of "talking to" to have any sort of meaningful relationship. I know now that there is nothing attractive to a man about a hot mess of a young woman when he is looking for a partner to spend his life with. Nothing about a girl slamming back shots in destroyed denim high-rise shorts, a crop top, and sky-high wedge heels screams "MOM MATERIAL".

At the time I thought I was the shit, and that everyone should want to be around me... Alcohol has that way of fueling your ego sky high. I was so desperate for attention, especially from men, that I put myself out there at all times and in any way I possibly could. I couldn't understand how someone as awesome as I thought I was was still single. Who wouldn't want to date the life of the party? Most respectable, driven young men looking for a future... that's who.

The first time this concept of "wasted time" hit me was at the wedding of one of my girlfriends that I had known for years. She had hired myself and my company to get her and all of her bridal party ready at her house that day, and it had been such a fun morning. She had been with her fiancé for years, and he was such a great man. I was so excited for them to become man and wife because he truly loved her so much. I had RSVP'ed to bring the guy I had been kind of seeing up until this time, but things didn't work out between the two of us. The hairstylist I ended up bringing with me instead had to leave early because she was running a marathon the next morning. I thought that I would be fine staying by myself at the wedding for a while. I knew a bunch of people that would be at the wedding, so I thought that I'd be fine on my own. The part I forgot to mention so far is that two of my exes would be at this wedding...

The one ex-boyfriend at this wedding was from years ago. I must have been around seventeen years old when we dated, but he was THAT ex-boyfriend... The one you still think about years later. The one you wonder how things would have been different if you hadn't been so young and dumb. The first one you truly loved in the deepest way you had ever felt so far in your life. I knew he would be there, and I knew he was now engaged to his long-time girlfriend, whom he started dating after me. The bride had also tried setting me up with her cousin years ago, which didn't end so well when he chose someone else over me. He ultimately ended up marrying her and divorcing her rather quickly. We had briefly reconnected, but I was still bitter about what had happened so it never went anywhere again. I knew he would be there, and that he now had a girlfriend too. It wasn't like I wanted to be with either one of them again, so I wasn't worried about seeing them and yearning to be with them. I just knew I was going to have to see them both and wasn't sure how it was going to go for me.

The cousin was very nice to me and said hello. I saw his pretty new girlfriend and they looked happy together. We were adults about the situation and it was totally fine. But then there was THAT ex… he acted like he had no idea who I was and didn't even look at me. I had planned on exchanging a friendly hello and congratulating him on his upcoming wedding, but he wouldn't even make eye contact with me for me to be an adult and do that. I made eye contact with his fiancé once, and I know she knows who I am, but he never even looked my way one time. I suddenly felt a wave of emotions coming over me. Within minutes it became clear to me how uncomfortable and upset I was. I sat there looking at my friend who had just gotten married, at the cousin in his happy new relationship, and at THAT ex with his fiancé, and all of a sudden I said quite loudly in my head *'I wasted SO much time.'* Here were all of these people from my past looking happy with someone else, moving forward in their lives together… and I had accomplished none of these things in my own life.

I began to have an anxiety attack sitting at the table, so I got up and made my way to the door, holding my phone to my ear like I was taking a phone call. Of course, I called my mama, and when she answered I said, "Talk to me while I walk out of this wedding…" as I made my way towards the door.

"I knew this was going to be hard for you," she said, and I felt the breathing get heavier and the tears start to well up in my eyes as I walked through the parking lot to find my car. She begged me to come over but I assured her I needed a little time alone. I drove around with no real destination after I stopped to pick up a pack of Marlboro Lights. I had dabbled in smoking socially while drinking over the years, but I would never say that I had been an actual smoker at any point in my life. Now that I had no alcohol to drown out my feelings, I would occasionally buy a pack of cigarettes when I was having an anxiety attack or a meltdown and chain smoke several of them in an attempt to calm myself down. That's exactly what I did on this night. I drove around in tears chain smoking my cigarettes and thinking over and over again about how all of those people were happy and finding someone to spend their lives with, while I had wasted all of my time partying. They were all happy and moving forward in life and then there was me... I tried reaching out to one of my sober friends I had made in England because we related on many topics like this, but with the time change he was asleep. So I drove and I smoked and I cried.

I eventually caved and went to my mother's house after she begged numerous times. She told me how unbelievably beautiful I had looked for the wedding, but at the moment I didn't even care how I looked. I calmed down talking to her and eventually went home. I tried to reflect and think about the evening a lot that night in bed and I was able to come to a more positive realization about my thoughts and feelings towards it.

I kept focusing on this idea that I had "wasted" so much time, but I had to look at it from a different angle to feel better about it. I hadn't wasted any time, it just wasn't MY time yet. I had to take the path I took to become the person I was now becoming. If it had been meant to happen for me already then it would have already happened. It wasn't God's path for me at this time, and the Universe hadn't perfectly aligned the stars just yet for me to reach those places. I became more accepting of the realization that my journey just wasn't the same as everyone else's, and that is totally okay. I had to stop comparing myself to others and thinking that I should be on the same path as them, because my path in life had been nothing like theirs had been.

I have truly began to believe now that everything that has happened in my life has been one little stepping stone and puzzle piece that will build together a bigger picture. Had I not been such a mess maybe I would have gotten into a serious relationship that lasted at a younger age. If I had a normal relationship with alcohol maybe I would be welcoming my first child into the world right now. If I hadn't been so stuck in partying for so long maybe May 25th would never have become a date that has such a significant meaning to me. I wouldn't be sitting here right now writing a book, that's for damn sure. Every little part of my life and every little choice that I have made along the way has brought me right to this. Every stumble along the way has brought me to realize the gift that I now have to share with others.

Hitting rock bottom gave me the words and the experiences to share my story in hopes that I can offer some sort of hope and strength to others. I was brought to this point to show that you can come back from your breaking points, you can change your life, and you can rebuild your story. I was saved and turned into the person I am now to prepare me for great things in my life, and to share my story with others.

It's so easy to feel like you are missing out when you compare yourself to others, and I'm telling you comparison is SUCH a dangerous thing. You can compare where you are in life to others, you can compare what you have to others, and you can compare your achievements to others, but who is to say that their path is right and yours is not? Everyone's course in life will twist and turn and wind them down millions of different roads. No two people will travel down the same road at the same time. I have learned how important it is to realize that when I start to feel down about the things I have not done yet in my life. There are a lot of things that I thought I would have accomplished by now, but there are also many things I have done that I never thought were possible.

While I may have "wasted" time when it came to dating and settling down in my twenties and most of my young adult life, there are so many things I have accomplished. Focusing on the things you have rather than the things you do not have is such a powerful approach to life. I guarantee you will be a whole lot happier when you look at it from that way. During my "wasted" time I have graduated with a college degree, and I have earned my cosmetology license. During my "wasted" time I have started and ran an award winning business and have started a side hustle on social media through my YouTube and Instagram.

The things I have gained during my "wasted" years that hold the most value to me are not actually things at all. I have found so much value in discovering my true friendships. I have rediscovered the relationship I had with my mother when I was just a young girl and she was my best friend. I have learned how to hit rock bottom and to pick myself back up. I have learned how to take defeat and struggle and to turn it into power and strength. I have been able to gain things that I consider to be far more valuable than any of the things I had "wasted" my time not doing. Of course my mother is still constantly on my back about when I'm going to give her grandchildren, because that's just your mother's job once you start getting older.

Is this where I thought I would be at 28 years old? Absolutely not. If you had asked me when I was young, I'm sure I would have woven you some bullshit fairy tale picture about being married to a handsome, successful young man, with a few babies on the way, in a beautiful white-trimmed brick house. I would have a home-cooked meal on the table every evening for a family dinner together and talk about how our days went. The dogs would be playing out back with the kids in the summers while they ate colorful popsicles in their bathing suits with the sprinklers on. I imagined I would have this perfect little cookie cutter life where all the pieces would just fall into place perfectly.

Somewhere along the way as you grow older you come to the realization that most of the time things just don't happen that way at all. Things get messy, things don't work out, and things fall apart. If you don't learn to roll with the punches you will end up very, very disappointed somewhere along the way.

So I'm in a place in my life now where I've had to accept the fact that having any sort of timeline for my life just has to be thrown out the window. You simply cannot try to plan out every detail in your life and when it will happen. There's just no way to predict if or when those things will happen. I've learned to stop waiting for things that might never happen, and to just live in the moment.

For a long time, I still held on to this idea that I had to end up meeting a significant other for things to start happening for me. I kept thinking that once I found someone else to share my life with that everything else would just fall into place as it was supposed to. I've been hesitant to buy a place before I meet someone because then I would be stuck with a place I'd have to do something with if we got married. Now I've had to come to the realization that I'm getting damn near close to 30 years old, and I can't lean on that idea anymore. Because of the path my life has taken, I may be buying my first place on my own. Because of the road I have gone down, I might not have children by the age of 30, like I had always hoped I would. Things in my life may end up extremely different than I had ever expected them to be, and I've had to learn to just accept it and roll with it.

Of course, there was a period of time where I had a hard time comprehending this idea of just letting things happen naturally. It was especially hard when all of my girlfriends started getting married and having babies. It was pretty much impossible to compare my life to theirs and not feel like I was falling behind. Although 28 is not that old to many people, when you're 28, it sounds extremely close to 30, and 30 is a huge milestone in your young adult life. I'm not sure why 30 carries such a heavy presence. Maybe because all of the other milestone birthdays like 18 and 21 carried new privileges at each age. With each of those ages I had felt like a little bit more of an adult because I was given more privileges (like being under 21 years old had ever stopped me from drinking before). I guess for me, 30 just carried some sort of stigma, and the possibility that I may look into getting Botox for the first time.

9 | DEAR MAMA

A lot of people say "my mom is my best friend" when talking about the woman that brought them into this world. I have always said this about my mama even though we've been through some pretty rocky terrain… To be honest we've been through monsoons, mudslides, tornados, and any other chaotic thing you could imagine figuratively. But at the same time we've been through sunshine, rainbows, tears of laughter, and every sweet sunrise type of scenario you could describe as well. No matter how high or how low the highs and the lows have been, she has never walked away and she has never turned her back on me. I can imagine there were many times it would have been the easy way out to just wash her hands of me, but she never did that.

When I was young, my mama was my everything. She only worked part time so she could stay home and raise my brother and me. My childhood is overflowing with memories of baby pools with sprinklers splashing into them, eating pigs in a blanket on a plastic picnic table on the driveway, riding my tricycle to the corner and back while she watched from the porch, and kitchen walls covered with our numerous arts and crafts projects. My childhood was the greatest, mostly in part to my mama.

We weren't rich, but we were definitely spoiled. She constantly surprised me with the newest Barbie, the newest Mary Kate & Ashley

VHS tape, and anything else I ever wanted (within reason). We went to Disney World on vacation as a family numerous times. We rode our bikes around Mackinac Island every summer. We spent days at our cottage on a small lake near Tawas, MI. Life was simple and life was good with my mama.

During the school year, whenever we had a half day, I would lay out my outfit the night before and paint my nails to match it before bed. I would plan out all my accessories and lay them out all ready to go. When the bell rang around lunch time, I would run out to the car where I would change out of my uniform in the backseat. My mama and I would go to Macy's to have Maurice Salads with iced teas for lunch and spend the day shopping together... she always called them our "special days". It was our time to spend together without anyone else. Life like this was perfect in the eyes of the little girl I was back then.

Typical teenage rebellion set in of course as I got older. As I hit the age of puberty and started to turn into a pre-teen, I didn't want to spend as much time with my mama. I would much rather be with my friends being rowdy and meeting boys on their bikes that lived in the neighborhood. I wanted to have sleepovers at other girls' houses and stay up all night laughing. I did still remain somewhat close to my mama during this time, but I surely started being a little asshole to her sometimes as well.

She never stopped doing anything I needed her to do or giving me any of the things I needed, regardless. No matter how many messes I caused or how many times I screwed up, she was always there to help me fix it in any way that she could. Even though I called her a bitch once around the age of sixteen and she tackled me down the floor, she was still the first one to show up when I called her to come get me when the cops showed up at a party. I never texted her back to let her know I was alive at 4 am when that's all she ever begged for me to do. Regardless, she was still the one that always made sure to leave a slice of bread and water next to my bed the next morning.

Some people might say my mama was an enabler, which I can totally see their point. She let me get away with way too many things in most people's eyes. She let me have friends over when my dad was Up North almost every weekend. Most of the time she probably suspected that there were bottles of Boonesfarm being chugged at the age of 15 in my bedroom with my girlfriends. She knew when I said I was spending the night at Natalie's that I probably wasn't there. She knew I was getting into all kinds of mischief at all hours of the night in Detroit. She knew I was at warehouse parties downtown practically half naked.

I will say that while everyone else was hiding things and lying to their parents, I never did that with my mama. She always knew the shit I was getting into. I'm sure she wasn't happy about it and wished there was something she could do, but in a way I have never thought that the way she parented me was "wrong" in any way, shape, or form.

Everyone has their own style of parenting, and a lot of people may say hers was not "right," but one thing I would tell them is that I never felt like I ever had to hide anything from her. She knows every mistake I have made, and every fall I have taken. There is something to be said about being able to be entirely yourself (good or bad) and having a relationship where you know whole heartedly that the other person accepts you for everything that you are. Maybe she should have locked me in my bedroom, maybe she should have grounded me and taken my phone away… but never once was our relationship a bad one. Not for one day of my life. And I think that says a lot about the bond we have shared over my 28 years of life.

The day I came home from the hospital really showed me just how deep the love of a mother truly runs for her own child. I would have expected her to be so furious with me. I expected her to not want to see me or have anything to do with me until she calmed down about it. Instead, she took me in with open arms. I was in such an emotionally fragile state of mind after what had happened, and she could see that. She did not yell or scream at me, she simply took care of me. She made her bed up and sat in the chair next to it and watched movies while I tried to get some rest. I know I made the comparison earlier in the book, but it really was like the scene of a first-time mother checking to make sure her baby was breathing while she slept. She stayed right by my side, and any time my body had a little spasm or jerk (in result of everything I had taken) she was right there reaching over with her hand on my leg asking if everything was okay. I was still her little baby no matter how grown I was. I was hurting... and she was hurting because she knew her baby was hurting.

We talked a lot that day... about everything. I knew something had to change. I had screwed up before, but this wasn't like all the other little screw ups. This one was big. I could be dead. It wasn't a chaotic weekend I could laugh off after it had passed, this one could have ended everything. This one could have taken a daughter from my mother. We discussed how this couldn't be taken lightly, that this was it and something would need to change. This time, I wanted to change. She told me that I needed to stop the way I was living, and I knew she was right. I was 26 years old and still a hot ass mess in many ways. I will forever have so much love for my mama for this day. For taking me in her arms regardless of how big I had screwed everything up this time. For always taking me for all that I am or all that I have been, whether it was good or bad.

Mama, where do I even start when it comes to an apology? I was always a handful, and I know that. You told me many times that you hoped that one day I would have a daughter just like me so I would understand what I had put you through... and now, I somewhat get it. Although I don't have any children of my own yet, I can only try to understand what I put you through looking back. Now that I am sober I see things a lot more clearly, and I can see plain as day, a glimmer of how you must have felt every weekend. I always rolled my eyes being the typical teenager that didn't want to listen to the woman that was raising her. I didn't want to listen to your rules. I didn't want to do the things you told me to do. Now that I am on the other side of things all I can start with is… I'm sorry.

I'm so sorry for the times you stayed up at night calling and texting me while I didn't respond because I was unconscious on a couch at a stranger's house. You were trying to make sure I was simply alive. You were begging me to just send you a simple reply text so that you could stop worrying and go to sleep, and I couldn't even be bothered to respond to reassure you of anything. Sometimes I would respond with a few misspelled words and a variety of random letters, and I'm sure those 4am illegible texts didn't help to calm your nerves very much either. I didn't care because I was selfish and only cared about my having a good time.

I'm sorry for the times you and Dad had to carry my limp, almost lifeless body into the house when I was handed to you on the front porch. I can only imagine how angry and disgusted you must have been carrying me upstairs to my bedroom like that. You probably were praying that the neighbors weren't awake and seeing your mess of a daughter. I'm sorry for the times you had to tuck me into bed with a pot next to my pillow just in case I woke up vomiting in the middle of the night. The amount of times I woke up to a cold, metal pot against my face while tangled up in my sheets wearing half of my outfit from the night before was ridiculous. I'm sure the fact that you had to do that regularly must have made you so angry. I'm sorry for the time I called you to pick me up from a party when the police came. I can't imagine how disappointing it must have been to watch your sixteen-year-old daughter take her first breathalyzer in front of you, and then be handed a ticket for underage drinking. I could go on and on about all of the situations I'm sorry for putting you in. But I don't think you want to relive all of them again.

I am a little thankful that as I got older you weren't always around to see as much of the trouble that I got into. You are such a kind-hearted, wonderful person and it would have truly broken your heart. This was the only time in my life I found myself wanting to hide things from you and be secretive, because never in a million years did I want to hurt the woman who cared for me with everything in her soul. It should have spoken pretty loudly to my conscience that I was starting to hide things from the person I felt like I never had to hide anything from. I knew I wasn't living in a way that was fair to the people that cared about me, but I just simply wasn't ready to face it yet.

I never intended to disappoint you. I never intended to break your heart. I never did any of those things intentionally or in a malicious manner. If there was anything in the world I could take back now, it would be those moments when I was breaking your heart.

Coming full circle with our relationship now, we are the best we have ever been. My getting sober brought back your little girl. It brought back summer mornings on the porch drinking coffee and talking, special days shopping and Maurice Salad lunches, trips to Vegas just us two to eat every delicious meal in sight and see the mountains… We are back to Mama and her best friend again. A lot of girls are close with their mothers throughout life, but I like to think that nobody has a relationship like ours. Maybe it's because of all the hard times we had to get through, maybe it's because of our general enjoyment of doing things together, or maybe it's just because we have a bond quite unlike any other.

So thank you, Mama. Thank you for never turning your back on me. Thank you for making sure I always had anything I needed in life. Thank you for helping me pick up the pieces. Thank you for supporting me in every crazy venture I've thought up in my life. Thank you for always being my biggest cheerleader, my shoulder to cry on, my everything. I know I couldn't have made it through these last two years without you. I love you forever and always.

10 | LOVERS & FRIENDS

One of the most difficult parts of the transformation my sobriety has sent me through has been adding and subtracting people from my life. Every idea I had about who was good for me, who I needed, and how deep my friendships and relationships ran ended up being shook to the core. It's a really funny thing to see how the people around you change when you change your life for the better. I've heard a quote many times regarding this idea, something about looking to see who doesn't clap when they see you succeed at something. When life happens and reality is thrown at you without hesitation, you really do start to see who claps and who doesn't. I definitely started to see who was there and who wasn't anymore. When major changes in your life occur it really can show you the true colors of those that are standing around you faster than you ever thought possible.

I have already talked about how I have always been a social butterfly, and that's an understatement. My outgoing, personable demeanor has always enabled me to start a conversation with just about anyone, anywhere, at just about any time. I can strike up a conversation with the old lady behind me in the checkout lane at Target, or even the mean spirited man waiting for his carryouts taking too long at the local Mexican restaurant. I talk a lot, I can talk about just about anything, and I just have that friendly effect on weird situations. We used to laugh at work about how I would end up talking to the most unpleasant customers and they would end up smiling and laughing after they were rude to every other person in the store. My mother is the exact same way; we have just always been very pleasant, friendly people that do not judge anyone. Instead, we strike up a conversation and turn any situation into a positive and enjoyable one. Life hands us lemons, and we always make lemonade.

I've always had a large group of "friends" throughout my life. I'm using quotation marks around the word friends because life has a way of slapping you in the face with harsh realities about the relationships you thought were the strongest ones sometimes. I've always had a big group of girlfriends that I invite over for every birthday or celebration. We could spend hours sitting around eating nachos and drinking "mockaritas" while piled on my sectional and faux fur bean bag chair having girl talk all evening. I have always loved being social and entertaining, and yes, I was being serious in that previous chapter when I said that this past birthday I did throw myself a birthday party including a nacho bar with "mockaritas" minus the tequila. I go all out for events. I even had sliced limes in my big, glass drink dispenser and salt to dip the rims of the non-alcoholic drinks in. Nothing makes me more excited than sharing time and smiles with the people that mean the most to me.

So going back to the quotation marks around the word "friends"… Ninety percent of the people that I spent every weekend with for years slamming shots, taking selfies, and passing out on couches with… Well, now I haven't seen them or talked to them in quite some time. Some of these people I haven't seen or talked to by choice, while others I fought so hard to maintain what I thought was a meaningful friendship with. It was like a cold drink thrown in my face to realize that the friends I thought were my ride or dies, the people I thought I'd have standing up in a bridesmaids dress next to me on the day I say "I Do" didn't seem to feel the same way about me anymore.

Some of them were easier to let go than others, because I knew that some of my "party friends" were just that… friends that were around for the party. Some of these friends were easy to identify as people that no longer offered me anything positive in my sober life. I never hung out with these people watching movies on a Sunday afternoon, ate pizza in sweatpants with them after a bad breakup, or called them crying when something went wrong. I knew these people were around when the good times were around, and I knew that they weren't deeply rooted in my life. Those were the easy ones to let go of.

The heartbreaking part for me was watching someone I considered to be one of my best friends drift away. I will be the first to admit that I clung to this particular friendship like an insecure little girl in a manipulative relationship. I made myself look like a fool trying and trying and trying to keep the friendship being what it had been before I had stopped drinking. I had shared so much time with this person, and she had been there for me through some of my worst moments in life.

I think that was what made it so hard to accept the fact that we were growing apart... the fact that she had always been there. We were always there for each other through the good and the bad, no questions asked. It started slowly, but over time became clear that this friendship wouldn't pull through and would not last through all of the changes in our lives. Priorities change, things change, and my life was not at all what it used to be. I continued for months to try to maintain our friendship until one day I was so hurt that I realized there was nothing there for me anymore. It broke my heart. I still hope that maybe one day the road that friend is on might bring her back to the friendship we used to share together. Right now it is not a healthy situation, it is not a good influence, and I need to move beyond it. I pray for that friend all the time that they don't end up having to learn things about life the hard way like I did.

The group of women I am blessed enough to call my friends now (minus the quotation marks) are some of the most amazing, caring, and inspiring women I have ever known. Some of them were around during the time I had my issues with alcohol, and I am so thankful that they were always able to see past the drunken mess to see the real me. I appreciate these women for never turning their backs on me and for being the most supportive people when I first embarked on my new sober life.

Some of these women are newer friends and some of them are people I have just grown closer to since becoming sober. Having a clear mind and a better perspective on life gave me the opportunity to see these women for the positive things they had to offer. They offered words of encouragement, praise for my accomplishments, and they were genuinely happy for me when good things happened to me. They have never been jealous or catty, worried about who looked the best in their outfit, or focused on who got more attention from men. They have genuinely been there for me as friends, and I am so grateful for each and every one of them.

I used to think spending time with friends meant getting all dolled up and going out partying. Now spending time with my friends has taken on a whole new meaning for me. I go visit my two friends with babies born within the last year at their homes often. We sit around watching Netflix movies in sweatpants drinking Starbucks while the babies crawl around on the floor. I cannot wait to have babies of my own, so my ovaries are literally crying and screaming at me the entire time I'm bouncing these cute little nuggets of love on my lap. I go out for brunch with new friends I've met through work, and we devour a stack of pancakes or french toast while we talk about the things going on in our lives. I go out to lunches and to the movies on a Sunday with the girls, so we can squeeze in some girl time on the days we all have off.

Going out to dinner with a friend has still been one of my favorite things to do. Sitting back, laughing about whatever funny things have happened lately, and sharing some amazing food is one of my favorite past-times with my friends. I look forward to making dinner plans with my girlfriends, and I usually go out at least once a week with one of them. While I look forward to it so much, I can also tell you how much I secretly enjoy being home by 9pm on a Friday night now too.

While I have been able to hold onto a close group of friends, I have also found myself making new friends along the way. At work, through social media, and everywhere else I have been able to connect with a ton of new people during my sobriety that I am so grateful for. I never thought I would be ending my twenties making new friends because I just always assumed you had already made your group of friends in life by this age. Boy, was I wrong about that one! I have befriended clients of mine, mutual friends, coworkers, and even made some amazing connections through social media. I even spent my New Years Eve ringing in 2017 with new friends, the friends of my cheating ex-boyfriend. That's right, I was invited and he was not. There's your karma for you. I had a blast ringing in 2017 with my "party water" (water filled with fruit-filled ice cubes- so cute!) in hand with this fun group of new friends.

Finding a tribe or a "Girl Gang" as my favorite author, Cara Alwill Leyba refers to it, is something that I have found such happiness and fulfillment in. I have found such a love for women coming together to empower and inspire each other. Having the support of your girls is something so rich and valuable in life, and I cherish it so much now. I am in several female empowerment and inspiration groups on Facebook, I listen to podcasts, I read books about it and I absolutely thrive off of the idea of women coming together to make each other stronger.

There are so many more factors I look at now with the people i let into my life. I want the people I bring into my circle of friends to be sincere, compassionate, and supportive. I want friendships that feel like family, not just people you're with during the party. I want girlfriends I can sit around with over breakfast and coffee, laughing and sharing whats new in our lives. I want a girl gang and a tribe of women around me that empower and support my every move in life. They are the ones that clap when I post a new blog, a new YouTube video, or win an award with my company. They are the ones I can call or text when I need to vent without judgement. I am lucky to have found a group of women that are all of these things to me. I am lucky to call these women my friends.

Dating… Ha! Where do I even start when talking about dating and the kinds of relationships I've had since getting sober. Thanks to Match.com, Tinder, Bumble, and any other technology driven dating website or app, I've done my fair share of sober dating. Oh, how interesting it has been, to say the least! I could write another entire book on the topic, and I'm often tempted to do so.

You get a whole range of responses when you tell someone you're sober in the dating world. Some people are totally cool about it when you tell them you don't drink. They literally do not care at all. Some men have told me it's "so sexy" that I'm drinking water and not getting drunk at the bar. Some refuse to order a drink while out to dinner on a date in an attempt to be respectful. While I appreciate the consideration and sensitivity, it really isn't necessary. I'm not going to burst into flames if I am within ten feet of an alcohol beverage. For myself, being around alcohol actually proves to me that I am strong enough to be around it and not want it.

But back to dating… Some people want nothing to do with you when you tell them you're sober. They might even "unmatch" with you on the apps so the conversation literally ends right then and there. When that is the route they take, I am actually thankful that they showed me upfront that they cannot handle things in life that are not easy and perfect, because life is not easy and perfect. Who needs a man that is going to chicken out and run away when the going gets tough? Not this girl!

Some men pay no attention to the fact that you are sober at all. Sure, they acknowledge it when you tell them, but that same guy might proceed to go ahead and order four vodkas on the rocks just during the appetizer portion of the meal. Maybe it is because they just don't understand your past issues with alcohol, but I will say that there was definitely no second date with the guy that got wasted before dinner made it to the table on his first date with the sober girl.

Some guys don't know how to respond to my being sober, and they can be pretty awkward about it. I have woken up to drunk text messages from a guy I hadn't even met yet telling me that I just can't be with someone like him "because you don't drink." So let me get this straight, because I don't drink anymore, I could never possibly be around someone that drinks… HELLO, THAT IS WHAT I'VE BEEN DOING FOR THE PAST ALMOST TWO YEARS NOW. Again, I am actually thankful for his ridiculous text message in the middle of the night to show me that I do not need to be with someone who has that mentality about the best change that I've ever made in my life.

The best way that I've experienced someone handling my sobriety during dating is that they acknowledge it, are accepting of it, but act normal regarding it. I never expect someone to not drink just because I am around, ever. It is not their choice, it is mine. They are free to live as they do, and like I said earlier, I have learned to be around people that drink because being around it is inevitable.

Just because you don't do something doesn't mean that other people around you won't do it too. I have grown to be pretty easy going about the whole situation. I've even driven a guy's huge pick-up truck back from a bar where we saw his friend's band play. Was I annoyed? Not at all. We had been on several dates and he had never once been sloppy or drunk in front of me, or disrespectful about it in any way. That night he had a few beers while enjoying a band at a bar, which is totally normal for a guy in his late twenties to do. Like a boss ass bitch, I climbed up in that pick-up truck, giggled while I moved the seat all the way up because there was no way I could ever reach the pedals, and I drove us home. You learn to adapt to situations in a positive way because it will be impossible to avoid them entirely. Like I said, it is my choice and my new life, and I don't expect someone else to jump on the bandwagon just because this is the road that I've chosen to take now.

When it came to men, I had been shallow and overly concerned about looks and physical characteristics primarily in the past. He had to be over six feet tall, he had to be in shape, he had to dress well… All things that don't really add up to equal anything important when looking for a partner in life. That is how I ended up with alcoholics, divorced fathers of three, and insecure bodybuilder types. Of course you need to be physically attracted to someone that you consider being with for the long haul, but those things should never be the ultimate deciding factors on whether you pursue a relationship with someone or not. Being young, drunk, and immature, I would pick out someone at the bar that I thought was "hot." I would always try to make it work or try to "fix" them. Call me naive, but I always held onto the idea that deep down inside of everyone they were generally good people. I thought that everyone could change and everyone had a good heart somewhere inside of them. I was very, very wrong.

My past relationships and the men that I dated were all disasters, with a few small exceptions. Looking at things from such a physical approach, I ended up manipulated, cheated on, and abandoned time and time again. Men I thought I was truly in love with had no problem laughing at me two inches away from my face while I cried after a fight. Men I thought cared about me reassured me numerous times "it just happened once, it will never happen again" when I found a Facebook message from a random blonde saying that she had taken a pregnancy test when he left it open on my laptop. Men I thought meant the deep, meaningful things they said to me broke up with me over a text message two days before a cruise we were supposed to be going on, only to use our plane tickets to take their ex-wife to Florida (hopefully third time is a charm for that re-marriage). I can see now that there was a pattern that ensued from all of these shallow, lust-driven relationships, and nothing about it was healthy or good at all.

Now that I am in a totally different state of mind, I look at people and potential partners from a completely different angle. At the beginning of this year at church the preacher talked about new year resolutions, and he told us to write in the notes on our cell phones not just a resolution, but what we hoped to do or accomplish in the coming year. I wrote in my phone "to love freely and be loved for all that I am." This could be interpreted in a number of different scenarios, but to relate it to dating in particular that is exactly what I am waiting for and looking for.

I want to love freely. I want to love in a way that is natural and not forced in any way. I want to experience the deepest and purest kind of love out there. I want to be loved for all that I am. I have compromised things about myself in the past to try to make things work with certain men. I understand that relationships take compromise. This is something that is hugely important, but should be done in a healthy way. When I say that I want to be loved for all that I am I mean that I want someone to love and accept me for every part of me. I want someone to see my strengths, my flaws, my quirks, my bad habits... and love ALL of me.

I went through many stages during these first two years sober when it comes to relationships. There were times when I wanted to just be left alone. There were times when I would go through episodes of depression and anxiety where I would go to work and come home, looking forward to just being at home by myself more than anything else that day. I pulled away from all of the people in my life in general. There were times I just couldn't put the fake smile on and make it all look okay, and during those times I just wanted to be left alone. Being alone gave me time to think, time to heal, time to grow. I didn't want to explain what was wrong over and over again, because sometimes I didn't really have an answer for what was wrong. Sometimes it was easier to just give myself the night off from people. Sometimes it was easier to give myself the time to heal from whatever it was that I was dealing with.

For quite some time I always had both Tinder and Bumble apps on my phone. I would spend an unhealthy amount of time swiping left or right through hundreds of men everyday. I think I had it in my head for a while that as long as I had someone in my life romantically that things would fall into place and just make more sense. I spent a lot of time searching and searching for someone that sparked my interest. I met some great guys, and I met some complete assholes. I won't lie to you: at the time I am writing this I have those apps on my phone again, because I just cut things off with another guy I had been seeing the past few months. I feel like I am in a vicious cycle of meeting a guy, dating them, finding red flags, and dropping them. Sometimes, I worry that this is making me become less emotionally connected to others and unable to form genuine connections of love. Just call me "Little Miss Baggage."

I know the men of my past have left some major scars on my heart and it makes me even more careful of who I let into my life now. I just hope and pray that I will be able to feel love for someone again, entirely and completely. But I also have to be very aware of someone's true colors when they start to show them and not be blinded my the infatuation stage at the beginning of a relationship.

I had been searching for so long for things to make me feel whole again inside. For a long time I kept looking for them in other things and in other people, men being my biggest focus. As I mentioned previously, in *Spirit Junkie*, Gabrielle Bernstein talks about how she had been treating men in her life as a sort of "idol" that she had to look up to. She talked about putting others above herself like they were better than her, and feeling like she needed to make them happy and keep them around.

This type of codependency in relationships is something I can definitely see in my own life. I immediately identified with her need to have overlapping relationships to cover up the underlying fear of being alone because I had been doing that too. By keeping new relationships back to back without much time in between, fear had no chance to surface. When one relationship would end I always felt the need to find the next one. I was always thinking in the back of my pretty little head that once I met "the one" everything would just fall into place and be perfect. This is such an unhealthy way of thinking to put so much worth in finding someone else just to make everything okay, and it is one I still struggle with to this day if we are being completely honest.

In my codependent habits, I always did one of two things… I either stayed with people I knew were not right with me for the fear of being alone or I RAN. It is kind of like the fight or flight mentality we have heard about in school. I have realized that more recently I haven't been fighting at all, I have just been RUNNING. When I see something I don't like or something that I think might be a sign that a guy in a relationship could hurt me, I run away as fast as I can. I shut off all of the feelings and the emotions and I run as fast as my little, perfectly-polished feet can carry me.

I have fallen into this defensive, self-protective habit of running away before someone else has the chance to hurt me for most of the second year of my sobriety. I no longer stay with people that are not good for me and I no longer let people that say they care about me hurt me. I have just been running away before anything can happen instead. I do worry about doing this because it almost feels like a sense of relief and safety when I just cut things off and run away. I no longer have to fear getting hurt or look for signs that this person could do me harm. I am instead thinking that I have just been able to avoid it altogether. In reality, this is also not a healthy way to go through and deal with relationships, and I am well aware of that. I cannot run from every little thing that might hurt me, because I would be running away from everything in life. So don't worry, I'm working on it.

Breaking this self-destructive habit of always looking for something to go wrong and then running away is going to be a hard one to break. After experiencing so much pain and hurt from past relationships it has just become such a big habit of mine with men. After reaching a year sober I felt so rebuilt and so grateful that I found myself being extremely overprotective of my heart, body, and soul. I have been given this second chance to change my life and the thought of someone hurting me again is absolutely terrifying to me. I never want to feel as low and as terrible about myself as I did at my lowest points, and it makes me have that impulsive instinct to protect myself. I still struggle with it. Someone I was seeing recently started to change the way they were acting towards me. I was in tears obsessing over the thought that he might hurt me after I opened up to him so much so early on. Ultimately my gut was right, and he played me real good. He told me every little thing I wanted to hear only to drop me like I was nothing after he got what he wanted. Learning to love again and learning to trust others again is definitely a work in progress for me, but I am taking it one day at a time.

What I've settled on now when it comes to dating is that there are certain things I am looking for in a partner in crime. I need someone who supports me and all of my crazy ideas. I need someone who wants to hear all about how my day went. I need someone to laugh at all of my silly and quirky jokes. I need someone to bring fun into my life. I need someone to love all of me, and not try to change who I am. I need someone who can acknowledge my struggle and my journey, and wants to help me to continue on it. I simply want all of the things that any girl wants... and deserves. Every girl deserves to feel so loved that their heart could explode. Every girl deserves to have a best friend as a partner. Every girl deserves to feel beautiful and like the only girl in the room. That is all we all really want in love.

I am getting older and I worry that I am not going to meet anyone anytime soon. I worry that I won't start a family and have children when I originally planned to in my life. But the thing I try to focus on now is that I simply cannot plan some of the things in my life. I did not plan to take this path to sobriety. I didn't plan to be single at 28 years old. I didn't plan on starting a business, and I surely didn't plan on trying to write a book. God (or the Universe, whatever you believe in) has a plan for all of us and if it is not our time for a certain thing to happen, well, then, it just ain't gonna happen. I find great comfort in the quote "what is meant for me will not pass me," knowing that whoever is meant to come into my life will come into it eventually, exactly when they are supposed to. I have to learn to appreciate and enjoy the journey along the way, no matter how many unexpected twists and turns it might take.

As I clung to my past identity in the difficult beginning months of my sobriety, I wanted to cling to the friends, types of men, and the lifestyle that I'd been used to as well. The longer I've been sober the more I am able to be aware of what I want from the people I let into my life now. I look for different qualities in the friendships I keep or welcome. I look for different things from the men I consider opening up to.

For now I try to take it day by day. I fill each day with people that make me feel whole. I fill my time with people that make me feel loved. I appreciate each and every one of the people that are in my circle of friends and I make sure that I give myself enough time to see them regularly. I do miss some of the people that I used to include in my circle, absolutely. But through these first two years of sobriety I've realized that focusing on having people in my life that will add to it in a positive way is now one of my top priorities. I may learn things from the people I meet or date along the way, but if they are not a positive addition to my life I try not to spend too much time on them. I simply try to fill my life with the most amazing people that I can. One day that might include a man, but for now it is a bunch of wonderful, compassionate individuals that I am blessed to call friends.

11 | WANDERLUST

I drove my small, red rental car down the length of the rocky shore, parked, and then took off my Nikes and my socks. I made my way towards the most beautiful lake I had ever seen in my life. The water was clear and crystal blue, and it felt so cool against my skin. I looked around to see mountains stretching up around me in every direction. As I walked along the edge of the water and looked around, I was instantly brought to tears. I couldn't believe how beautiful this place was and I couldn't believe that I was here.

I was on vacation alone after doing destination wedding makeup in Nevada, seeing the most beautiful place, and I was ALIVE. Had I not walked out of that hospital after that night on May 24th, I wouldn't have been standing where I was in that moment. I wouldn't be feeling the cool water on my skin or taking in every little thing around me. These were the moments that always hit me the hardest after I started living sober. When I was surrounded by beauty and alone with my thoughts, I was reminded just how lucky I was that I had been given a second chance to live. That overwhelming feeling of gratitude still brings me to tears every single time, no matter how much time has passed.

The best thing I discovered along the way during my first two years sober was my ever-growing and passionate love for travel. Sure, I had taken many trips throughout my life. Growing up, I went on multiple trips to Disney World with my family and a handful of other places during my childhood. I went on spring break my senior year of high school to Panama City Beach, which if you've learned anything about me so far, you know that that was just a shitshow of playing "Hey Mr." to get alcohol, destroyed denim Hollister mini skirts with sleazy tops, and taking body shots off of strangers on the beach. Several of my single girlfriends and myself went on a booze-fueled cruise through Mexico and Central America a few years ago, and we partied so hard that most of us were actually physically sick after the five-day cruise ended and docked in Miami. Sure, I was traveled as a young adult, but never did I travel like I would after becoming sober.

I went on a few small trips in the beginning of my sobriety. I visited places like Chicago, Orlando, and all the other typical, touristy locations around the U.S. Around six months sober when that one serious relationship ended three days before we were set to go to the Bahamas for my birthday, my mother dropped everything to take that girls trip with me to Vegas. This was the first trip that would really reveal my love of traveling to its full extent. Of course we had a blast being in Vegas. I had never been there so everything was new and exciting to me. My mother suggested we get a rental car and drive out of Vegas to go see the mountains in Zion National Park in Utah, about a three-hour drive away. Now let's take a moment to remember that your girl is a makeup artist, never leaves the house without her lashes on, and the only thing she's ever climbed is the sale rack at Nordstrom's.

We got in our little, white rental car and of course detoured to stop at a Starbucks. We set out on the drive and listened to music while singing along during the three hour drive. When we reached Zion, I was immediately overwhelmed by the size and beauty of the mountains that began to stretch up around me everywhere I looked. I had never been anywhere like this before and I had never seen such incredible beauty in nature.

We spent the day exploring the easier trails. We saw half frozen waterfalls (we were visiting in February), all kinds of animals in the wild, and cliffs that my mother was too scared to walk out on, while I eagerly took selfies at the edge. I was so overcome with feelings of excitement, happiness, and almost a sort of "high" if you will. The type of excited, overwhelming "high" I had once gotten from partying I had now felt again but in a more healthy and fulfilling way. I had never done anything that made me feel this way before, and I was loving every second of it! It was like when people joke that they are "high on life," I literally felt this way while I was traveling and discovering new places. After feeling that type of "high" again, I wanted more of it. Had I finally found the ultimate healthy replacement for partying? All I knew was that I loved everything about the feeling that traveling gave me.

I complained in therapy that year that I wanted to travel more but that none of my friends were ever able to get the time off work or had the money to go. My therapist simply looked at me and said "so GO." I looked at her with no response for a moment. She pressed on asking why I needed someone else to go with me to go on a trip and I sat there thinking, "she's right." I decided that day that I would look into my first solo trip that I could take in the next month or so. For some reason Savannah, Georgia has always been intriguing to me. I'm not sure if it was the Southern style of living, the cute Southern guys with accents, the thought of the amazing BBQ food, or being near the coast that drew me in most, but I decided this would be a good first trip for me to take by myself. I didn't want to go balls to the wall crazy and go somewhere international or too daring for my first solo trip because as excited as I was about it, I was still a little nervous too.

So I did it, I booked the trip and that was that… I was going on my first solo vacation. When my flight arrived in Savannah I got my rental car and I was off. It was nowhere near as scary as I thought it would be. I had booked the most perfect little bed and breakfast in the heart of the walking squares just outside of Downtown Savannah. I fell in love with this place! It was a two-story Carriage

House behind the main building. It offered a fireplace, claw foot tub, and a balcony overlooking the gardens where I enjoyed the most delicious breakfast and coffee every morning. I spent my days with my country music blaring and the windows rolled down while I "island hopped" along the coast to Tybee Island, Jeckyl Island, and anywhere else I hit along the way. I walked barefoot along the most beautiful beaches. I drove down winding backroads lined with hanging moss covered branches like something out of a movie. I wandered through wooded areas of thick moss covered trees and branches as the wind gently swung them back and forth. I sat on a bench looking around as tears welled up in my eyes… as I realized I could have missed this.

After the two disastrous relationships I had just gotten out of, it was safe to say that I trusted no man at this point. On this solo vacation I was in a very "YOLO" (you only live once) state of mind, and coincidentally a guy I had matched with on Tinder back in Michigan was in Georgia working on a movie set at the exact same time I was there. We decided it was too coincidental to not meet for the first time ever in Georgia, so we made arrangements for him to drive to Savannah from Atlanta where he was working. He told me he had never seen the ocean and I immediately said we were going to see the ocean.

It's one of those random, Universe-driven moments in life that you never forget… Here I was walking on the beach barefoot at midnight with a guy from Michigan who happened to be here the same time that I was. We spent the entire next day of the trip exploring islands together and seeing the most beautiful places. It's funny because we have never seen each other again since that trip, but we still stay in touch via social media here and there. At the time it was exactly what I needed from the Universe to show me again that there are genuinely good people in the world. There were still genuinely good men out there.

Not only did that happen on this trip, but when my flight got delayed and I missed my connecting fight home due to storms I got stranded at the Atlanta airport until the following day. Normally, I would have been so stressed and annoyed by this huge inconvenience, but a guy my age that was flying from Atlanta to another state for a wedding also got stranded. We immediately became friends and ended up having a sleepover watching movies on my Kindle lying on the floor and sleeping in a corner together in the airport all night. I swear, only these things happen to me in life. In the morning he even bought my breakfast and waited with me until my flight boarded. People on my flight were laughing after he left saying they had thought he was my husband, because we were having such a good time. The two of us laughed so much, made the best of the situation, and it was yet another person placed directly in my path by the Universe to show me that there are genuinely good men out there, and that I didn't need to have my guard up for every person who came my way.

The entire trip left me feeling stronger, inspired, and with a whole new outlook on things. There were so many places I still wanted to go. There were so many things I still wanted to see. I had almost missed out on all of these things because of alcohol… I would have never seen the mountains for the first time, walked barefoot in the most beautiful lake surrounded by mountains, and explored those beautiful moss lined backroads leading to those coastal islands had I not changed my life and started my journey in sobriety. The feeling that travel gave me, that indescribable "high" I felt, and the richness it left in my heart was something I wanted so much more of.

I was already brainstorming my next trips I wanted to take when I got back from Savannah. This trip changed so much for me that it is almost indescribable. I have a shell that I took from one of the islands along the coast in Georgia, and I keep it in a little cubby in the center console of my SUV. Sometimes when I'm driving, seeing it reminds me of how strong I can be and how much that first trip on my own introduced me to one of my biggest passions in life to this day.

Since that first trip I have taken a few more solo ones. I also started advertising my business for makeup for destination wedding jobs, and the first one I booked took me back to Las Vegas. On this trip I decided to visit Red Rocks Canyon, El Dorado Miner's Ghost Town, the Hoover Dam, and Lake Mead. I can't even tell you how many times I cried during this trip, and not only because it was that time of the month and the hormones were running high. I cried in Red Rocks because of the overwhelming beauty as I drove through the mountains, because it hit me once again that I could have missed all of this. I stopped with fellow travelers to help a tarantula cross the road (Yes, that happened.). Lake Mead was one of the most breathtaking places that I accidentally stumbled on, and I walked around in the water surrounded by mountains in total awe of the natural beauty around me. I cried again there like the hormonal young woman that I am. I can't help but get so overwhelmed sometimes by the thought that I could have not walked out of that hospital alive and wouldn't have been standing where I was at that very moment.

Traveling for weddings has taken me to Charlevoix, New Buffalo, and all over the state of Michigan and parts of Northern Ohio. Being in new places with new people all the time is something I absolutely love about what I do for a living. The opportunity to travel while doing what I love has made me feel so blessed, fortunate, and thankful that I chased after my crazy dreams to do this. In the next coming year I will be traveling to a few more spots for work trips, some even internationally! It's so exciting getting to travel to places for work that feel like a vacation, and I always take advantage and stay a few extra days to explore the new places I get to go. Fingers crossed that someone decides to take me on their destination wedding to somewhere insanely beautiful like Bora Bora. Heck, I'd probably die of happiness if someone even took me to Hawaii right now! Baby steps, baby steps... All in due time.

My family has had the cutest little robin's egg blue cottage right on the mouth of a small lake in Northern Michigan ever since I was a baby. It is nice and cozy, but nothing super fancy. It is a small cottage about the size of someone's apartment, but it has the most beautiful views and is surrounded by nature. Thinking about growing up spending summers on the lake, I think of buckets full of frogs, playing in the sand at the nearby beach, and endless amounts of mosquito spray. I remember my father raking leaves into big piles that my brother and I would jump into. I remember boat rides and going for walks with my mama to see "Swamp Thing" which we had said was the monster that lived in the swamp back in the forest… Life was great. I am so grateful that I had the opportunity to grow up spending so much time in this place, our little home away from home.

As a preteen and teenager, I hated going to the cottage. I was at the point where I wanted to be with my friends and the thought of a family vacation was the least appealing option during my summers. You had little to no cell phone reception up there, no internet, and no boys. Well, no boys that I wanted to pay any attention to. Once I started partying, the cottage became even less appealing to me. I would have much rather been at whoever's house didn't have parents home that weekend carrying bottles in my purse from whoever had bought my alcohol that night. I seriously loathed going to the cottage for years at this point. My mother did allow us to bring up a group of friends once, and we had an absolute blast. We were drinking while having bonfires and boat rides. There were three people passed out in every room, and also in a tent outside. I can remember us girls smoking a pack of clove cigarettes thinking we were totally badass at the beach. The cottage was fun again to me during that trip, and only because my partying lifestyle from home had come up there with me.

I rarely made it to the cottage throughout high school and college, and I rarely went up in the years following that. But, after getting sober and discovering my love for travel, the cottage took on a whole new meaning for me. I went up north during my first year sober and it showed me a new beauty that I had never noticed or appreciated before. The water was just a little bit clearer and the trees were just a little bit more green. Wandering down wooded paths and across wooden bridges was filling in some of the parts of my heart that had been broken for so long.

I took my little Kaya in to town and we played in the sun at the dog friendly portion of the beach. We even shared a little picnic lunch by Lake Huron, just the two of us. Things had become simple again, just like when I was a child. I could enjoy the simple things of this place again. I could enjoy the simple things in my life again. I have been up to the cottage several times during my sobriety and wish I could make it up there more often. Adult life has come along with a laundry list of responsibilities that don't make it possible as often as I'd like. But now I always make sure that I block out a few days a few times during the summer to get up there as my mini escape.

When I worked my wedding up in Charlevoix in Northern Michigan last fall, I stopped at the cottage on the way up and on the way back. I took Kaya with me and left her at the cottage with my father, who basically lives up there full time during the summers. It was such a great trip... Not only did I get to do makeup for a client and friend of mine up in beautiful Charlevoix on the water, but I got to see more of the state that I hadn't explored before.

I have never appreciated our little cottage as much as I do now. It is such a simple, small place but it represents so much to me. It represents a simple life, an innocent life, slowing things down, and taking in the beauty of things in the world again. It's my own little mini escape just a few hours away that I have grown to absolutely love, just like I did when I was a sweet, innocent, young child so many years ago. I had rediscovered my love for this place that has been such a big part of my life growing up. I loved the cottage again. But, my desire to travel more always had me looking for new places to go.

I am still a little uneasy about traveling international by myself. I am only five feet tall and if I get stuck in a situation straight out of the movie *Taken*, Liam Neilson will be nowhere around to rescue me. So, I continued to start small with my solo traveling adventures. I had never been to California, so Cali began calling my name next for an impromptu birthday trip.

I made it to California, my first time on the West Coast! I fell in love with everything about California... except for the traffic. Staying at an Air Bnb for the first time, I had the most adorable little apartment down the street from the beach in Marina Del Rey on the coast. With the horrible time change (I swear I never adjust to it anywhere), I was falling asleep around 9 or 10 PM and waking up by 6am everyday. I decided to take full advantage of it and would wake up, put on some layers, and walk to the Starbucks down the street with my headphones plugged into my iPhone. Every morning on the trip I had my morning coffee watching the sunrise over Marina Del Rey from the Pier. It was simply perfect. These mornings gave me so much time to reflect and relax. It was another one of those times in my life where I just felt so grateful to be standing where I was, doing what I was doing. There I was coming up on 2 years sober with a New Year's Resolution to travel and see new places more... and I was doing exactly that. I was on a solo vacation in California in awe of the sunrise and the fact that I was doing exactly what I had made a resolution to do.

Driving up the Pacific Coast Highway 1 in California is a memory that I will never forget. I drove for hours up the coast and saw so many beautiful sights along the way. I saw mansions in Malibu worthy of a Kardashian. I saw hills of vineyards as far as the eye could see. I saw groups of people working in never ending fields of crops on both sides of a dirt road I cruised down. I explored trails on the coast and hiked the hills, and I explored some of the most beautiful beaches along the way.

Every time I go on one of these trips I can't help but feel a little more badass, a little stronger, and a little richer in life. I have become this young woman that changed everything about her life and was doing everything she wanted to do now. With my sobriety, I was able to create this amazing life so full of experiences. I would have never done any of these trips had I not hit rock bottom and started down this road of self discovery, and for that I am forever grateful.

Now I realize that there are so many places I have yet to see and so many things I have yet to experience. I finally got my passport, and now my mind wanders to the incredible places internationally I will explore next. I can't wait to make it to Europe, Italy, Thailand, and everywhere else along the way. I daydream about tropical beaches and rainforests. I think about trying the most delicious food in new places. I think about learning about new ways of life other than my own. I think about living every day of this life to its full potential, and really truly seeing everything I could have missed.

When I look back at my past and think about my experiences with traveling so far, I can only think that I wasn't truly living before this. I may have been having a good time, but there are so many things I have learned that I truly cherish and enjoy more now that I am sober, including travel. I have made my life feel so much more full, rich, and complete with every day that passes.

12 | EMOTIONAL OVERLOAD

So let's get one thing straight, being a female is just an emotional overload at times by itself. Am I feminine enough? Do I want children? I wish I had bigger lips. Should I get a boob job? Are my friends talking about me behind my back? Should I change my hair color? I should work out more. It's that time of the month. How old is too old to have babies? I should try online dating... OH MY GOSH. I guarantee at least some of these have run through any girl or young woman's head at some given time during their life. Sometimes it feels like all of them are rushing in at the same time. Throw some hormonal periods in there and *BAM*, a cocktail for an emotional breakdown. Pass the chocolate, the chick flicks, the carbs, and the tissues... because we as females carry a lot of weight on our shoulders (physically and emotionally).

When I was wasted every weekend, I tended to not think about things as much. I saw it as a release from my problems, my emotions, and pretty much everything else in life. I could drown every worry, every care, every stress of my day away with shot after shot after shot after shot. This was such a routine for me that I didn't realize I was doing it regularly until I stopped. Obviously I knew I was getting wasted every weekend beyond the point of recognition, but it was not until I was deep into my sober journey that I realized just how much of a role pushing away my emotions had played in my drinking. I thought I was getting drunk to have fun, to get dressed up, to laugh with my girlfriends, and to meet new people. In reality I was using alcohol as a means to drown out a lot of things about myself and about my life that I didn't want to deal with, my emotions being one of them.

I guess I should have realized from my rocky preteen years that when it came to mental health, emotions had a huge role in my life. I was a happy, smiling, fun girl that everyone wanted to be around, so it was unfathomable for me to think that I didn't always have emotional stability. You would have thought the cutting and the pills would have shown me that early on, but I thought it was simply teenage angst at the time. My ability to just block things out as I got older was a trait that I thought made me strong, resilient, and unstoppable. I thought I was a badass because while every other girl sat at home crying after a breakup, I would be out on the town living it up. I would be in a brand new outfit, looking amazing, getting all the free drinks I wanted, and meeting new men. In a way it was like a big "F YOU" to the guys that hurt me. In my mind I was thinking, *'Oh yeah? You thought you could bring me down?'* and posting a bunch of selfies looking amazing to show them that nothing could break me. But the reality is that it is normal to break down, it is normal to hurt when things go wrong, and it is normal to feel things. I had way too much pride to accept this idea back then, so a Saturday night out was my answer instead.

When I first decided to get sober, it was almost like being around my friends and around partying was my own screwed up way of making myself face it head on. I wanted to prove I was strong enough to be around alcohol still, but not actually need it. Not the most recommended approach to sobriety by anyone you could ask out there, I'm sure. But that's how I had always been, and I always did things my own way. So I faced this demon head on, physically, mentally, and emotionally. Let the rollercoaster ride begin!

I was feeling lost, confused, and downright broken, but I was trying to hold it all together so nobody would see that. I knew it would be hard for me, but the extent of how hard this would turn out to be emotionally was something I could have never prepared for.

I didn't realize just how much I would break to the core emotionally while I was navigating my way through living sober. I never knew how much I would discover about my own emotions and the way I handled them in my everyday life.

In my dating life, my emotions had grown to be very disconnected over time. I was able to walk away when a guy did one thing wrong and I was able to ignore the people that hurt me. But, deep down all I wanted was someone to be with. I wanted someone to love me so badly that I was desperate for anyone that showed me they would. I've pieced together in therapy that the rocky relationship I often had with my father growing up probably played a huge part in this. I wanted someone to approve of me and the things I did. I wanted someone to be around. I just wanted someone to give me love for exactly who I was.

I would throw all of my insecurities into my relationships with men. I went above and beyond to make sure I gave them my all, and time after time it seemed to always get thrown back in my face eventually. I wasn't choosing the right men to be with, yet I would try to overwhelm them with my love to make them be the men I wanted them to be. I'm sure you can all piece together by now that this never worked for me, and it would never work for anyone else either. It's like a movie plot from your typical romantic comedy with the girl trying to save the bad boy, the guy from the wrong side of the tracks. My dating life had turned into an 80s chick flick reminiscent of Molly Ringwald ending up with that guy in detention with the leather jacket and the fingerless gloves in *The Breakfast Club*, expect it didn't end like the fairy tale I was hoping for.

I never cried. If I cried people knew something was REALLY wrong. When I think back to all of my teenage years and early twenties, I rarely cried at all. I was too stubborn, too strong, and too prideful to show my emotions like that to others. Fast forward to today, and any YouTube video of soldiers coming home to surprise their kids or their dogs sends me into a total meltdown.

In the past I never let my emotions show like that. Of course, I cried when there was death, when I was really hurt, or when something was life changing… but I rarely let my emotions out. I don't know where I attained this idea that letting out my emotions and expressing them was not okay. I think I was just so stuck in the idea of being a strong and resilient young woman proving everyone wrong that I felt like I should hide my emotions and not show any signs of weakness. I wanted to seem unbreakable.

When I nearly died on May 25th 2015, I didn't begin to process the emotions of it fully until the following day. Even in the days that followed, I was absolutely numb. I cried, and I cried a lot. I cried in a way that I was barely feeling anything. I did not feel strong, I did not feel empowered, and I did not feel unstoppable. I felt like I had been broken to pieces. I felt like I was lost.

Going through those feelings and emotions was one of the hardest things I've ever had to do. When I think of my first 365 days sober, I think of a lot of things. When it comes to the emotional side of it, I think of myself hitting the lowest of my lows and being broken down to nothing. I know this sounds mellow dramatic, but I am telling you I have never felt the dark and low points that I felt during this time. I had started out in my new sober life naive, hopeful, and determined. When shit started to really get heavy on me emotionally, I was a total mess. I had no idea how to handle any of these feelings and emotions, and as I've elaborated in prior chapters, I was grasping at anything I thought might help. I had been turning to church, men, and anything else to try to make myself feel whole again. When those men I had relied on so heavily were gone, I didn't know where to start when it came to facing my own emotions.

My mother and I went on that trip to Vegas and being on that trip distracted me from the feelings that I didn't want to deal with or face yet. When we came back I quickly made plans with my girlfriends to go out the next night because I did not want to deal with all of those emotions yet or the reality of everything that had just happened. I met that bouncer at the bar and a rebound relationship quickly ensued. He was emotional and in the process of finalizing a divorce. I was freshly left and an absolute mess.I was in no emotional state to begin another relationship.

I hadn't even dealt with the hurt, the pain, and the abandonment I felt from the last guy and I was simply pushing all of my unresolved issues onto the next one. What ensued was one of the worst experiences of my life emotionally. I was not myself, I had lost all of my self worth, and I was letting someone drag me through the dirt along the way. When I think about this relationship it was like I had absolutely lost my mind for a while. My emotions were completely out of control and I was driving myself insane. He broke my heart numerous times and I continued to take him back. I let him beat me down again and again and again and again, and then he would manipulate me into thinking I had done something to cause it. I was such an emotional basket case by the time I finally got out.

All I wanted was for someone to love me. All I wanted was for someone to stay. I was so emotionally broken that I was willing to give up myself, my pride, and my self-respect just to not be alone. He put me down in any and every way possible. He was the landslide that led to my emotional rock bottom, and when I hit the bottom... I hit it hard.

There was a handful of times in my life that I look back on now and classify myself as actually being full blown "depressed." Not in a funk, not in a weird mood, but literally depressed to the extent that it interfered with my life. It took a very long time for me to actually admit that I live with depression and anxiety. Nobody wants to admit that there is something wrong with them, and I had felt weak in the past when I considered the idea myself. It wasn't until I was in therapy after these two relationships ended that my therapist made a comment referring to my being "someone living with depression and anxiety" that I actually accepted the fact that I DID live with these things. When she said it I literally thought, *'Wait, what?'* feeling a little blindsided by hearing the statement being said out loud so casually. I needed to hear it out loud like that from someone outside of my circle of friends and family to believe it. Once I accepted it, it became a lot easier to navigate my emotions. I was someone living with depression and anxiety and I had been in denial about it for a very long time.

That last relationship led me straight into depression. When I had finally opened my eyes after people I trusted were asking me what I was doing staying with this type of person, I realized just how much I had been letting myself get walked all over. I finally knew I had to walk away after the last time I took him back for cheating, because he actually got mean. Put down after put down had been thrown at me, like he was trying to convince me that I wasn't good enough. Emotionally, I felt like I was going insane. I felt crazy. When I finally woke up to this reality I thought, *'What the hell am I doing!?'* I remembered that strong girl that was still somewhere inside of me. She would never have put up with this. She would have told her friends to leave him numerous times if it was someone else in the situation, so why wasn't she telling herself that now?

I had to block his phone number and every social media account because he was trying to manipulate me into staying. He even emailed my business email because he knew it was the only thing that would go through. He tried to convince me that he loved me, as manipulative people often do. The bottom line I realized and I hope other women can realize is that SOMEONE THAT ACTUALLY LOVES YOU WILL NEVER INTENTIONALLY TRY TO HURT YOU. If I hadn't been strong and if I had given into the emotions, I would have let him back in. I was holding onto the last string of strength I had in me to keep him out. I knew I was an absolute mess emotionally and he had only made it so much worse. That little string of strength was somehow enough for me to ignore the blocked voicemails that continued to come through, to ignore his manipulative attempts to keep his claws in me… and somehow I did it. It was not easy and there were days I felt so low that all I wanted to do was go to bed to get to the next day in hopes the emotions would be gone, or at least less intense.

This became my telltale way to know when I was going through an episode of depression. I am one of the most active, driven, go-getter types out there. I am an overachiever and I try to fit way too many things into the hours of one day. For me to be wishing it was later so I could go to bed is so out of character for me that I knew something was majorly wrong. I cried for days...I cried on the way to work, held it together while working, and then cried on the way home. My mother finally persuaded me to have a girls' day with her to get lunch and go shopping. This had always been one of our favorite ways to spend our days off together.

I sat at the Arabic restaurant where I only ordered a bowl of lentil soup. On a normal day I would be ordering salad, chicken, hummus, bread, and eating way more than anyone my size should be able to consume. This day, I ordered just a bowl of soup. It sat in front of me and I felt like I didn't even have the energy to pick up the spoon. I took a few bites because my mother kept begging and pleading with me to eat. I barely tasted it. I barely ate any of it. I didn't even feel hungry. We went to our favorite home decor store and as I walked through the sliding doors my mother took a cart and turned back to look at me... I was breaking down into tears. I had no control of my emotions whatsoever. She handed me the keys and told me to go sit in the car. I sat in the passenger seat with my face in my hands, sobbing and staring at the floor mats. I was so lost. I was so broken. I was so empty.

I knew at this point something was radically wrong. This wasn't just a bad breakup, this was an emotional breakdown and I was depressed. I was in the midst of the worst episode of depression I have ever been through in my entire life. This was the first time during my sobriety that I didn't have someone that cared about me as a partner. The people I had put my love into had thrown in on the ground and spit on it. I was just a shell of a person navigating through the days. I was leaving work early numerous times. I was crying in front of customers. Something had to change. This was not me and I could not continue to live like this. This was the point when I finally took the first steps to find a therapist. I finally accepted the fact that this stubborn, strong, independent girl could not do it alone this time.

I had said many times I wanted to get into therapy, but until you fully decide you actually want to go for yourself you won't make the effort. Now I wanted to go. I wanted to end this cycle of depression and I wanted to learn how to be healthy emotionally during this difficult journey in my sobriety and in my life.

I wanted to understand why I drank the way I did and I wanted to know how to navigate these feelings. I had never dealt with my emotions in the past, I simply drank past them to not deal with them. When all of these emotions were rushing at me this time I didn't have alcohol as my outlet. The tornado of emotions swirling around in my head was so overwhelming at times that I didn't know what to do. Everything felt so intense and so amplified. Without the blackout to push the emotions out I was forced to face them head on, but I had no idea how to do this. I pulled away from people, I lost my motivation for my everyday responsibilities, and I hated the person I was becoming. It became very evident to me at this point that I had never dealt with emotions in a healthy way at any point growing up. I never expressed my emotions and I never let anyone see me in a vulnerable way. Learning to do this was one of the biggest accomplishments I have made in therapy thus far.

In these first two years sober, the episodes of depression have been more frequent. They happened a lot more often in the beginning, and were triggered easily by a lot of things. Over time I have grown to learn how I handle and work through these bouts of depression best. When I start to feel the tiredness, the numbness, the lack of life in my step, I mentally prepare myself for the funk I'm about to walk into. Sometimes the depression is just for a day, sometimes it is for days, and sometimes it's just plain unpredictable. I always try to mentally prepare myself for what I'm about to work through. While it may seem strange to some, I fully bask in the shittiness of my depression. I cannot ignore it, I cannot just brush it aside, but I have to actually work through it.

Ask anyone that has lived with depression and they will tell you that there is no way to just "snap out of it". People will reassure you that nothing is wrong and everything is fine, but depression and anxiety are not things you simply "snap out of". I have to mindfully work through it and it can be absolutely exhausting mentally.

After an episode of depression, even though I may not have even done that much physically, I feel absolutely drained. It is almost like I have to coddle myself back to a normal state of mind like a small, helpless child. I have to acknowledge what has triggered it and I have to accept it. I make sure I feed myself good food, I work out, and I watch movies or listen to music or books that I enjoy. I have also found that listening to self help or motivational audio books is extremely helpful to me during these emotional times. I enjoy sitting back and listening to uplifting words of support from others that have been through similar things.

Now don't feel bad for those of us that live with depression or anxiety. Even though it can be difficult and throw us off track here and there, I am so grateful now for feeling all of these raw, intense, and powerful emotions. Perhaps the main reason I don't absolutely hate that I have these episodes is because I am actually FEELING these emotions now, and it makes me feel more alive. Even though I'm feeling something that makes me hurt so much deep down in my heart, at least I am feeling it. After drinking away my emotions for years, feeling the hurt reminds that I am alive and that I am living. Even the bad times make me feel grateful because at least I am here.

I've read so many quotes about how you cannot realize what the good times are if you have never seen what bad times are. Without the pain, the struggle, and the dark times… Would I be as grateful and appreciate my successes, my growth, and the light and good things in my life as much as I do now? I'd like to think so, but I doubt it. Coming up on two years sober soon, I am now able to acknowledge and navigate my emotions without a drink or a bottle glued to my hand. I can now identify when I need to just be alone and have time to process my feelings. If something feels like its a little bit off, I take a night off to work through my funk. While it is still definitely a work in progress, sobriety has helped me to actually feel and handle my emotions in a healthier way.

13 | GOD, THE UNIVERSE, AND HIGHER POWERS

Now, I promise this chapter isn't about throwing the Bible in your face and telling you that you're wrong for not believing every word of it. Trust me, my own faith has been something that has taken so many twists, turns, and tailspins throughout life that I'd be a hypocrite to try to shove it down everyone's throats. God, Jesus, and the Bible are all things that have been studied, questioned, and questioned again. I can totally understand why people are skeptical about them. I mean you are asking the world to believe that a man was born from a virgin, that he could walk on water, and that he rose from the dead after they hid his body away in a tomb. You are asking people to believe that a man could split a sea with his staff and his hands, that Adam and Eve created all life, and that a talking snake told them about forbidden apples. Trust me, I get why so many people are skeptical about religion.

I was raised in a Catholic Church and I attended a Catholic private school until I was in the 8th grade. We went to church every morning, confession every Thursday, and studied religion every day as part of the curriculum. We wore plaid uniform skirts and had to kneel on the floor to measure how long they were to ensure we weren't rolling them up to make them shorter (such rebellious girls we were). I will be the first to admit that I only went along with all of these rules and ideas as a child because I was forced to do so. I wasn't comprehending half of what it all meant, but I am grateful for the early knowledge about religion and where it came from. I do think attending this private Catholic school instilled a lot of morals and shaped me behaviorally in my early years. At the same time, I also think it is very limiting and controlling for young adults.

I have mixed feelings about this experience in my life, and it ultimately led me to stop going to church once I was a teenager. My mother didn't try to force me to keep going, and I am grateful for the way she handled it. I would only come back to my faith and religion if, and when, I was ready to do so on my own terms.

When things would go wrong in my life, I would stop and pray about them occasionally. I didn't pray regularly, so it kind of made me feel like a phony. I definitely left my faith in the dust during my partying days. At no time during an alcohol-fueled night of debauchery did I stop to think that maybe I should go back to church or to thank God for watching over me. I can even recall at one point saying that when I got married I wouldn't do it in a church because I thought it would make the people I would be inviting uncomfortable.

I had this chip on my shoulder towards the church because I personally had an experience with a priest when I was a volunteer altar girl that wasn't the greatest. Altar girls or boys wore the traditional draped dresses and handed things to the priest or carried them away, basically an assistant during the service. One particular day the priest had made a joke to myself and the other alter girl along the lines of "You need to stop being so pretty or I'm gonna have to spank you." and tapped us both on our bottoms as we stood on each side of him. Let me tell you one thing, if you want to absolutely destroy a young girl's entire outlook on religion and priests, this was the perfect way to do so.

I felt so uneasy about what had happened that I told my mother about it and she immediately made me quit altar serving altogether. That experience made it pretty easy to lose my drive to go to church for quite some time. I later saw on the news that the very same priest that did that to myself and that other young girl was accused of touching a women when she was young, and he had fled to Florida. Reassuring, right? At this point in my life I was already far from my faith, so it was almost laughable for me to see it on TV.

I might not have believed in God or the Universe, but I do know now that He believed in me. During the sloppiest times of my life, I believe someone was looking out for me, especially during all the times I blacked out while drinking. Someone had to be. I made it out of way too many dangerous scenarios in one piece. I like to think now that God, angels, and the people I knew that had passed away were the ones watching over me and covering me with their protection. Do I know if this is definitely what happened? Not really, but I like to think that it played a role in keeping me safe for all those years.

Now here comes the crazy talk, so brace yourselves. My grandmother had a near death experience when she was a young girl where she was hit by a car in the street. I was still young when she passed away, so she never told me the story herself, but my mother has shared it with me since then because she felt it had great relevance to my sober life and the things I have experienced. After she had been hit by the car, my great-grandmother laid her in the bathtub while they waited for help to come. My grandmother swore to my mother with great certainty numerous times that she could see herself lying in that bathtub from above. She described being able to see her body and her mother crying at the bathtub like she was above them looking down on the situation.

Throughout my grandmother's life, she would have dreams about things happening before they had even happened. She knew my mother was pregnant with a girl when she first got pregnant with me. She even sketched a picture of what I would look like before I was born. She dreamt that President Kennedy was shot days before he ultimately died on that iconic day in history. She had some sort of intuition where she always had feelings or senses about things that were going to happen.

Cut to my situation and my experience, which was surely a near death one as well. Although I don't remember it, people that were at the hospital told me that I kept saying those remarks about angels and bright lights before I was fully stable and conscious. Was I just talking crazy talk because I was so messed up? Maybe. But I can't even start to explain to you how much more in touch I have become with my faith, my connection to the Universe, and how insane my dreams have gotten over the past two years. Call me a hippie, call me crazy, call me whatever you want, but I fully believe some dreams have meanings and signs from the Universe. My intuition and dreams have been so on point at times that it's given me some serious goosebumps. I like to think that I am somewhat like my grandmother now, and my mother is convinced that I am because we both shared near death experiences early on in our lives. We could just be absolutely insane, but it does make for some pretty crazy stories and coincidences in life.

I'd like to share with you a few of my crazier experiences with my faith, the Universe, and my dreams giving me amazingly accurate guidance. When I tell my therapist or my friends their jaws seriously drop. I even blew away a pastor with my one particular dream involving Jesus.

We'll start with the Jesus dream, since we've already covered the religion topic a bit. As I said previously in the book, my ex-boyfriend attended church with me when I began going again. He had told me about hearing God speak to you in life, but I had never experienced anything like that (and personally, I thought he sounded a little bit crazy). The night after I told him I wanted to go to church this is the dream that I had...

I was in a big house with a whole bunch of people. Everyone was acting really unkind towards me and making jokes about my being there. I felt so excluded and left out that I went outside for a walk and a woman began to walk with me. A little girl was following us throughout the dream. She was young with dark hair like mine and bangs. As I walked with the woman I shared with her how upset I was that nobody was accepting me in the house. I began to tell her about my past issues with alcohol and how I was trying to change my life now as we walked down a dirt path surrounded by grassy fields. Out of nowhere, a bull with one horn appeared, and the bull was bleeding. He charged me and bucked me up high into the air, and I fell back down to the ground. He was gone. She helped me up and we continued walking as a man with dark hair and a beard was ahead of us calling us back to the house. He called out, "You have to come back inside!" so we headed for the doors. I walked into a large room with a group of naked women in a large shower together. Someone called me over and told me that I hadn't signed in yet and I needed to sign in on the book he had on the table. I told him I didn't want to take a shower so he told me to just sign in for now. I wrote down my name and some numbers next to it, and we were called back into the large main room.

The man speaking in front of everyone announced "Because Sarah made it and is still here with us, both groups will get their gifts now..." He handed me a book and he handed the little girl with dark hair and bangs the other gift. I didn't even look at the book to see what is was, and I passed it on to someone behind me. The little girl approached me for the first time and said, "I'm going to give you my gift, because I know you won't give me yours." She began popping eight white figurines out of a plastic sheet, each one resembling a person wearing a gown with a tall hat. The man that had been speaking had approached us, and as I turned to look at him I realized that it was no longer the man that had been speaking in front of everyone. He was now wearing a white gown with a light blue sash draped over his shoulder. His hair was long and flowing, and a light was coming from within him. His lips sparkled with light as he spoke to me. It was Jesus that was standing in front of me, or at least the image of what I always thought he would look like.

I don't remember anything he said. I just remember being paralyzed in shock in the dream as he spoke to me. He walked away and up the steps onto a small stage to continue speaking to everyone. I was still frozen in absolute shock as tears ran down my face. He stopped talking, looked over at me, and made a motion with his hand telling me to wipe the tears away from my eyes. He whispered loudly to me, "Don't forget to smile." I woke up gasping for air, sobbing, and having a complete and total meltdown.

I sat in my bed crying so hard that I could barely breathe. I was saying out loud, "I'm gonna go to church" and "I'm so sorry" over and over. Some people might say that the only reason I had this dream is because I had talking about going to church, but I like to think it was the moment that I let God back in. I opened up to the idea of rediscovering my faith, and Jesus was in my dream to guide me back to where I needed to be. I needed to go back to the house, I needed to wipe away my tears, and I needed to smile again.

I researched the things I saw in this dream relentlessly, and I found a lot of Biblical connections to many of them. I discovered that the bull attacking me but my surviving and getting away could be symbolic of alcohol trying to kill me, but that I survived. The bull having one horn and bleeding could represent that part of my demon was killed, but part of it still remained to be destroyed. The house could be representing my returning to the church. The women in the shower could symbolize my baptism and being cleansed of my past. The little girl has returned to one other dream of mine since this one. In this dream she showed up at my workplace and she sat in the chair in front of me. She told me that she came to warn me, telling me that, "He's going to attack you." I'm still not sure what she was referring to. Some people have told me they think the little girl could be myself as a child, but I like to think that maybe it's the daughter I so badly wish to have one day giving me guidance.

I didn't realized it until just recently as I have been finishing writing this book, but there was a huge sign in this dream that I never noticed at first. Jesus gave me a gift in the dream, and it was a book. The moment I made the connection that the gift he had given me was a book, I got goosebumps all over and tears filled my eyes. THIS was my gift. The story you are reading right now was the gift that was given to me.

Something that has also come to me repeatedly in my dreams are warnings. They come to me in many, many forms and they always come when I am unsure about a situation, a person, or a decision in my life. I can almost count on these crazy dreams any time something is happening in my life where I need guidance or a sign. They have come to me as yellow scorpions with one claw, the bleeding bull with one horn, speeding tickets, the words of the little girl, and many other things. I always immediately Google my dream meanings as soon as I wake up before I have a chance to forget them. Time after time, I find that the meanings of the things in my dreams often reflect warnings or answers to things happening in my life.

Recently, a guy I had dated briefly reached out wanting to reconnect. We hadn't had a terrible ending to our somewhat relationship, and I had really cared about him so I was considering it even though I knew we disagreed on a lot of major issues. The first night I had a dream that a police officer got into my car and gave me a warning ticket. He told me, "This is the second warning ticket you're getting..." and stared blankly at me for a few seconds too long like he was trying to really make me understand something. Later in this dream I realized that I had prosthetic legs and was walking with special leg braces. I heard people talking about how my ex-boyfriend had shot me in my knees and I had to have both of my legs amputated (I know, I have some of THE weirdest dreams). When I woke up I had no idea what to think of this dream, but then I started to piece it together when I researched what the different things meant. The second warning was truly a second warning. The first time I had dated this guy I had a dream that my brother and I were trying to find a yellow scorpion with one claw hiding in a bedroom. Yellow is a warning sign in dreams, and scorpions represent trouble and problems.

The speeding ticket I received in this dream, my "second warning" says in dream dictionaries that it also directly represents warnings of things to come. When I looked up what it means to have prosthetic legs things got really creepy. Having prosthetic legs in a dream means you're trying to follow or do something in life but "deep down you know it's fake and it isn't real"... I had been questioning for days if he was being real with me or if this was all just him telling me what I wanted to hear to see if he could get me back. Wouldn't you know that he completely blew me off after that day, after pouring out his heart to me about missing me and missing us and wanting to see me again. He bailed on our plans and I never heard another word from him again.

That entire weekend I had dreams about amputees and people being paralyzed. I had another dream where a girl in a wheelchair that was paralyzed from the neck down told her family she didn't want to be a burden to them anymore, and then threw her body from a cliff. I screamed out as I watched her hit every ledge on the way down with blood coming out of her mouth. It was extremely disturbing. The following day I was doing a makeup trial for a bride whose upcoming wedding I had booked. When she arrived, I had to just about hold my jaw from dropping to the floor when I realized that one of her arms had been amputated. The next day someone direct messaged me on Instagram in a way that sounded like we had known each other in the past. When I responded and looked at his photos, I quickly realized that we had matched and talked on a dating app a few years ago but had never actually met in person. As I glanced at his Instagram feed, I instantly realized something about him looked very different... He had jumped off of a boat into shallow water sometime after we had first talked and was now paralyzed from the neck down and in a wheelchair.

I don't quite understand what all of those things with that common theme of paralysis and amputees means completely, but I somehow feel that it was warning me about the situation I was able to avoid for a second time. I just couldn't believe how it had not been subtle at all how these things were thrown at me one right after another. Call it a crazy coincidence if you want, but I don't think anything in my life is really a coincidence anymore.

If you start analyzing your dreams it can really be quite interesting. Of course, some people will think this too is crazy talk, but I love researching my dreams. Sometimes dream imagery just reflects things going on in your life, but sometimes I truly do take some guidance away from it. I've had dreams about hiking in Acadia National Park in Maine, which I plan to visit sometime in the next year. I've also dreamt that I was in Prague exploring cathedrals. Once I woke up I had to look up where it was on Google, because I didn't even know where Prague was. The day that followed I heard something about Prague three separate times randomly, so I like to think that this is the Universe telling me I should go to Prague one day and experience it. If you are open to experiencing these strange signs and coincidences, you surely will start to find them everywhere you look. You just have to be open to them and start looking for them.

I have read a few books by Gabrielle Bernstein about spiritual awakening, meditation, and being open to signs from the Universe during my sobriety. All of these books have helped me to be more open and accepting to these ideas. The entire idea to start writing this book came from signs that I like to think came from the Universe.

I felt an urge to share my story from the beginning, and that was when I began making a YouTube video on my channel for every milestone along my first year sober. At first some people watched and commented, but suddenly the views began to spike in number. A lot of people were watching and listening to my story. I began receiving messages and emails from people all over the world reaching out to tell me that they had a story like mine. People emailed me for advice and praised me for being open and honest about my struggles for all the world to hear. I began to have a stirring in my heart that I should be doing something more. The comments became more active on these videos, and I began emailing regularly with a handful of people about our sober journeys.

As I kept feeling the stirring to do more, I wasn't sure where to even start. I was a makeup artist and social media beauty chick. How was I going to do more with my story involving alcohol? Around this time I received an email from a production assistant at Dateline

NBC. They were doing a special about one of their news anchors who had battled alcoholism all her life. While looking for things to include in the special, they had stumbled on my One Year Sober video on YouTube. This was a mind-blowing moment for me. Someone had seen my video, had heard my story, and wanted to include a clip of it on a nationally broadcast television show on a major television network. Of course I excitedly responded, "YES!" and gave them the approval to feature a clip from my video in the special. It ended up just being a small clip in a montage of others during the episode, but it was such a huge moment for me. This urged me even more to do something to share my story, so I decided to start my blog and begin writing.

I had written in college and had always felt I was pretty good at it, but I had never had any practice writing a blog. After shuffling through a number of names and seeing what domains were available to purchase, I settled on "soberAF" and purchased soberAF.com. My mother had no idea was "AF" stood for, so I had to explain to her that it was slang for "as f***". I like to think that I can be serious, yet am able to be raw, witty, and humorous about my situation and so the name seemed fitting.

The first blog post I finished was titled *The First 365* and it outlined the first year of my sobriety. This was the first time I had publicly put everything out on the table about what had happened on May 25th, 2015 and everything that had followed it. For the first time I allowed myself to be completely open by sharing more details about the situation publicly than I ever had before. I received such a huge outpouring of support. It felt like a million pounds had been lifted from my shoulders. I knew I was being directed to the things I was meant to be doing with my story.

I continued doing blog posts regularly, but I still felt that stirring to do more. I talked about it in therapy often, about how I felt something telling me to do more inside my heart. I had seen ebooks online, but I didn't know the first thing about writing anything that substantial. I talked to the husband of a friend of mine, and he was very encouraging that I should just start writing short ebooks. I researched online how to make ebooks, how to sell them, and anything else I could find on Google. Although I was looking through it all, something just didn't seem right. I didn't know what to write about, exactly. Something just wasn't fitting 100% with me. When I feel this way I usually try to keep an open mind because maybe I am trying to force something that just isn't happening or evolving naturally for me. Then I had the dream...

I can't remember where I was in the dream, but I was in a large room and there was a small table to my left. There was something on the floor next to the leg of the table, so I bent down to pick it up. Upon getting closer, I realized it was a white book lying face down on the floor. As I picked it up, I opened the book to see a photo of myself in the pages. Glassy, distant eyes and disheveled hair and makeup stared back at me from the page. The picture was me. Wasted, drunk, and sitting on the floor somewhere. I was in my typical partying outfit, scantily clad to say the least. I was grasping a bottle in the photo and stared out blankly from the black and white ink. When I realized it was myself in the book, I flipped through several more pages. The whole book was my words, my story, and pictures of myself as the wasted young adult I had been for so long. The book I found on the floor was not just a book, it was MY book. I awoke from this dream with so much certainty of the sign I had just received. This was how I was going to share my story.

I've lost motivation many times while writing this book and for many reasons. When I have lost my drive to write or feel stuck I have doubted myself and lost confidence in my writing. I asked myself many times, *'Why am I writing a book?'* and *'What if nobody wants to even read it?'*. Since I don't know the first thing about writing a book and I'm just figuring it out along the way, I wasn't sure how to make chapters or how long they should be. I questioned how many pages I wanted to have. At times the way I was trying to write just wasn't flowing as easily as I felt it should have been. I got frustrated, and wondered if it was all just a big waste of time.

I started to notice that anytime I would feel this way, I would receive an email from someone saying they related to my story. If I was feeling defeated or like I should have been farther along in my writing than I was, I would get a very encouraging comment on YouTube thanking me for sharing my story. These acted as little nudges from God or the Universe in my eyes, as they kept me going to write more. On one particular day I was listening to *Bittersweet* by Sheila Niequist while running on the treadmill. On this day I had been feeling like I had really hit a wall with my writing. At the end of Sheila's book she repeated many times to "share your story." She says many times that your story is meant to be shared, and that you should go on and share it. As I listened through my headphones I knew that this was my nudge from the Universe that I was doing exactly what I should be doing.

This chapter may just be a lot of hippie talk to you. You may not believe in God. You may not believe in the Universe or any sort of higher power out there. There is something somewhat comforting and reassuring to me about there being something out there more powerful than myself. While getting sober I found that having my faith again and focusing on the spiritual things in my life helped me to reconnect with my soul again after it had been lost for so long. I did a lot of self-discovery along the way in this sober journey of mine, and focusing and learning more about myself spiritually has helped me heal along the way.

14 | MOVING FORWARD

Looking back on the past two years, I see they have been nothing short of miraculous, insane, and beautiful. Looking back at my entire journey, I can whole heartedly say that I am at peace and fully accepting of the idea that it was supposed to happen exactly as it did. I was meant to struggle through my teenage and young adult years, and to feel hopeless and lost along the way. I was meant to drunkenly stumble through my young adult life, and I was meant to end up in a hospital at 26 years old, which became a slap in the face telling me to WAKE UP. I had been given a beautiful life and I was wasting it away through my use of alcohol and partying. I had been given a life to live to its full potential, and I was not doing that whatsoever.

Although I would never have wished upon myself that terrifying experience where I almost lost my life, I am ever so grateful now that it happened. Had that night not happened and slammed the breaks on my life when it did, I'm not sure where I would be or what I would be doing right now. Maybe I would have been fine drinking my way through life. I would have never known the potential of what my life could have been without alcohol in it. I wouldn't have known anything about the woman I am now, so I surely wouldn't have felt like I could be anyone other than who I already was. I wouldn't have known the feeling of accomplishment I now feel when I think about my sober journey and just how far I have come. I probably would have been content continuing on in life the way I had always done. I pray that if I would have continued down that road that I would have never screwed up big enough that I ended up seriously hurt or dead, but I can't guarantee that that wouldn't have happened. Who knows what may or may not have happened if I'd not gotten that wake-up call. I can only say that I am just so relieved that I did go down the road I'm on now.

Now, of course, it seems insane that alcohol had to nearly take my life before I'd walk away from it. I can't understand how at no point during those years with all of that chaos and all of the warning signs that I never thought anything was wrong. Just like abusive relationships, you can never see what is happening when you are in the thick of it. You can only see these things once you have put down the bottle or walked away from that person when it is your decision to do so. Now, I just thank God for May 24th, 2015 because it was the best thing that ever happened to me. It was a terrifying and horrible experience, but it led me to new life. Without that night and the realization that there was another way to live, I would have never gotten to this place of self-acceptance, self-love, and rediscovery. I would not have the passion for everything good in my life that I have now. It is hard to describe the sense of gratitude and happiness I feel when I think about where the journey has brought me so far.

I have never been so accepting of myself and everything about me, and I have learned how amazing it feels to be more comfortable in my own skin and my own life than I ever imagined was possible. Some days, I swear I simply cannot wipe the smile off of my face or stop the sun from shining out of my ass, and that is such an amazing feeling. My life now on any given day has a sense of fullness to it, like it overflows with good things constantly. This overflow is the most beautiful overabundance of happiness and joy that I have ever experienced in my life. Even when I may be having an "off" day, I find it hard to stay in a negative frame of mind for very long anymore. My entire outlook on everything has changed, and it makes it so much easier to roll with the punches of everyday life.

My dating life has still been all over the place, but I haven't been in a serious relationship since the two I was in during my first year sober. I have been single for so long not because I want to be alone, but because I am now able to see all that I want, need, and deserve from someone else.

I no longer look for men just to have someone there. I am waiting to find someone who makes me feel alive again. I am waiting to find the type of man that I can't wait to see again every time he leaves. I am waiting to find the type of man that I find myself daydreaming about the amazing future we will share together full of love, travel, and a beautiful family. I am waiting to find someone that I can love freely without worry or fear, and someone who will love me for all that I am. I took a screenshot recently of a quote that made perfect sense to me in what I have been waiting to find, and it reads "while they all fell in love with her smile, she waits for the one who will love her scars". I couldn't agree with this idea more. I am waiting for the one that will take all of me, including all of my baggage and scars. They are still a part of who I am and always will be. These things have shaped me into the person I am today, and the kind of man I am waiting for will accept every single one of them.

Although the thoughts of my ego and the baggage of my past relationships are definitely not completely gone, I have been able to identify them better and not let them come out as much in my current relationships. Even recently there have been moments where I have found myself getting in my own head again thinking that something is different or wrong, when really everything is completely fine. It's like a little sliver of that self-destructive pattern of waiting for something to always go wrong still tries to fight its way back to the foreground of my mind. If I let my ego take control and let my mind run with it, I will even think, *"oh, well I could just move on to the next one like usual"*. Sometimes the thought of just walking away from the chance of getting hurt again seems like the safer option. It's times like these that I have to resort my mind back to love and the idea that not everyone out there is conspiring to hurt and abandon me like I had convinced myself in the past. If I hadn't learned to push this way of thinking out of my mind like I have started to do now, then I would probably always be waiting for something to go wrong so I could run away again. If I continued to live that way I would never be able to let the love of another person in completely.

The friendships and relationships in my life now are so near and dear to me. I hold these people so close to my heart and am so grateful for each and every one of them. I cherish every get together and every girls' night out (or in) that we share. My family and I are closer now than I ever remember us being. We even go to church as a family sometimes. We have not done anything like that since I was very young. Now I look forward to our weekly Sunday routine of church followed by going out to breakfast. The people I include in my life now and the relationships that I have are so strong and so important to me. I am blessed to have each and every one of them.

Becoming sober and navigating my way through the emotional and mental obstacle course that had been set up in front of me has been one of the hardest things I've ever done. There were times that I felt so hopeless and lost that I wasn't sure which way was up and which way was down. There were so many times it would have been easier to just let it all go, give up, and slip right back into my old ways.

The young woman I used to be has contributed a lot to this newfound sense of self of mine, but I think the past is a great place for her to stay locked away. I would never regret or change anything about one single day (no matter how shitty it was), because each day has been a part of the road map that has led me here. That road map has finally led me home again after such a long and difficult journey.

I have gotten so close to no longer looking for outside things to make me feel complete anymore. I continue to look inward and discover the things inside me that make me feel whole. I have always heard quotes about how "everything you need to be happy is found within you" and that you should "love yourself first." It has taken a long time for me to believe these ideas, but I am getting there. I love myself more now than I have at any other point in my life. I give myself all of the things I need and I take care of myself in all ways possible. I am learning to find everything I need within me and give myself the life I desire... and it is such a beautiful thing.

I continue to deepen my faith and my relationship with God with every week that passes. Sharing this with my family now has made it even more special for me. I like to think that God had this plan all along of bringing us back together through church. I still believe in higher powers and that there is something greater and more powerful than all of us more than ever. The Universe sends me more signs and guidance now than I could have ever asked for, and I am even more open to receiving them. Even while shopping around to find someone to do the cover art for this book, a woman sent me a quote of her pricing and some sample pieces of her work. I had previously envisioned the idea of an image of a tipped over glass being on my cover. Wouldn't you know it, one of the samples of her work she sent me was a book that had an image of a glass tipped over on the cover of it. Thank you once again, Universe. You never fail to steer me in the right direction when I need it.

Sometimes, I do worry about what happens if my sobriety comes to an end. Will I ever feel the need to drink again? Sometimes I still like to play with the idea that maybe one day I will be able to have a glass of wine with dinner while on a beautiful vacation somewhere amazing with my future husband. Would I slip back into my old ways? Do I have the strength and knowledge now to be able to drink in a "healthy" way? Maybe it is just the novelty of the idea that always keeps me coming back to it. It could be because old habits die hard.

I guess I really can't tell you what the future will bring in terms of my sobriety right now. I do know that along the way I was so worried about missing out on things when I gave up alcohol, and I no longer feel that way at all. I have come to see that I can still have amazing experiences and live every day of my life to the fullest without alcohol being a part of it.

On a date recently we were talking about how this particular guy I was seeing felt like because he socially drinks and I don't that something would be missing or weird about us being together. We laughed about how nothing about our time together is any different just because I happen to be sober. With the biggest feeling of peace flowing inside of me, I explained that I still enjoy every day of my life just as much as I ever did while drinking. It has been so amazing to get to the place where I can say that out loud with 100% confidence and absolute sincerity.

So I'm two years sober now... now what? I have no idea what is next for me and there is such an exciting lining to the undefined future that awaits me. Having an unwritten future can be scary at times, but thinking of all the possibilities of what it may bring gives me a sense of excitement and anticipation. There is so much potential for what could come next and where this journey will take me. I simply cannot wait to see where that will be!

Will I continue writing? I'm not really sure. I can say that while I am rereading this one last time before sending it off to my editor, I am so overcome with emotion. There were times when writing this book seemed nearly impossible and I was filled with doubt. Finishing it now, I know that when it is completely done I will surely cry my eyes out. Not only has it been therapeutic to relive all of the experiences and the emotions that came along with them, but it has also allowed me to gain closure on everything that has happened in my past.

Sharing my story has allowed me to meet others with stories like mine, and I have thrived off of the connections I have made along the way with total strangers. Every time an email comes to my inbox from someone thanking me for my YouTube videos or blog posts, I can't help but feel such a sense of love. To think that my little story and my little words could reach and possibly help people is so rewarding, and I can't wait to share this book with all of you when it is finished.

My hope is that at least one or two people will read my story and see a little bit of themselves in it. By seeing themselves in my story, I hope they can use this book to feel love, support, and to grow in their journey as well.

As someone once told me in an email, they found hope watching my videos of my first year sober. I was lucky to be given this gift and it would be selfish of me to not share it with the world. That is why I have invited everyone into my struggle so publicly. I want to inspire, to support, and to show others that they are not alone in their fight. If one person can read this and take something positive away from it to use in their own life, then this was all worth it. I welcome you to continue watching my journey, share this book with someone who may need it, and to listen to my words. I hope they give you support, comfort, and hope in your own journey... and don't forget to smile along the way.

EPILOGUE

Writing a book is f***ing HARD. I have grown to harbor a new-found respect for all of my favorite authors even more than I already had. You'd think it would be easy to just write. You'd think it would be easy to just let the words of every thought in your head just pour our naturally, but that is not how it goes. Numerous times along the way I thought about stopping this project of mine. A million negative thoughts of self-doubt almost crushed the entire thing along the way.

I worried that people would judge my writing harshly because let's face it, I've never written a book and it wasn't going to be written like that of a *New York Times* best-selling author. I worried that maybe I was putting too many details about my struggle out publicly, and that people might form new judgements about me as a person. WHAT IF NOBODY EVEN WANTS TO READ IT?! Would I feel defeated and like it was all a waste of time? A big thank you to all of the not so subtle nudges I received along the way from God and the Universe. Each one pushed me forward with a hand of encouragement, like a baby's parents holding their hands to help them stand while they try to take their first steps. After that first step, they will begin to walk, and after they walk they will begin to RUN.

I started writing this book on a flight to California, my first solo trip of this year. I had never been to the West Coast, I had never seen California, and I was just overly-excited about life at that moment. Something about sitting in my window seat with my little fruit cup typing away at the Introduction to MY FIRST BOOK seemed so surreal… but I loved the feeling. I thought about how I would respond to the man in the seat next to me if he asked what I was working on. "Oh I'm just working on my book…" How BADASS would it make me feel to say that out loud!? Very. Those thoughts of self-doubt still remained throughout the writing process, but I think that's just normal when you're doing something completely out of your comfort zone for the first time. The most I had ever written were college papers, and even those ten page assignments seemed like they were never ending.

I was able to keep myself on track by allotting myself a block of writing time every day. I found that waking up an hour earlier on most days and dedicating it to writing helped me out immensely. I would wake up and feed Kaya, make my coffee, and just start writing whatever came through on that morning. I would dedicate a certain amount of time to writing with my big mug of Cinnabon-creamer flavored coffee. I found that doing this first thing in the morning gave me a clear head since I hadn't taken on the day yet. I was more able to let the feelings and emotions and words just flow. At first I tried to write in an extremely structured manner but I quickly realized it didn't feel natural and nothing came out as freely as I thought it should. So I started jumping around and writing in chapters when I felt like I had something to write about. That's when the writing got easier and things started to flow more.

This journey has been amazing, but it's also been hard. I've had to stop writing in the middle of a chapter because I could feel myself going back to the emotions of that time as I relived the moments. Reliving some of the most difficult times of my life through writing has forced me to face them head on again. I've even slipped into a slight depression here and there while writing this, but I continued pushing on no matter what.

My ego wanted to doubt me over and over but I had to convince myself that at the end of this I will have written a book… I WROTE A F***ING BOOK! Even if nothing became of it and nobody wanted to read it, can you imagine the sense of accomplishment I would feel upon finishing an entire book? That is such a "check it off the bucket list" type of thing. It would totally be a female empowerment moment for me, that's for damn sure! So the first thing I want to share in conclusion of this book is to never, ever doubt yourself in any way in life!

Find your spark, share your passion, and chase after every dream you have! Do not ever let someone tell you that you cannot do something. No dream is too big for you to reach. Open yourself up to all of the possibilities of the things you can accomplish when you put your whole heart into them.

I have noticed that people that share sobriety in common tend to stick together. I have witnessed first-hand how when I find someone who's sober, it is like you share this undeniable connection instantly. You share the same struggles and obstacles in life, and you have finally found someone else who just gets it. There is a huge sense of community in the sober world. I have encountered some of the most inspiring, supportive, strong individuals along the way as I have shared my sober journey on social media. I am hoping that this banding together of the sober community will help this book to spread my words around to those that may be needing to hear it. My ultimate goal is that this book will be passed around and will help people like me.

My hope is that my story will give others hope that they too can change their life for the better and rediscover themselves along the way. The way I saw the sober community band together as I started to share my story is what has inspired my numerous videos, blogs, and even this book. We are all just one big, dysfunctional family of f***ed up people trying to make it through this life on our own little twisted path.

For all of the people out there struggling with alcohol, drugs, sex, depression or any other type of addiction… YOU ARE NOT ALONE, AND YOU NEVER WERE. There are dark times when surely it feels like you are nothing, you have nothing, and there is nobody out there for you. Find that one thing that makes your heart beat. Fight harder than you've ever fought. You were given this life to live it, and you should live the shit out of every damn day of it.

ASK FOR HELP. I tried being stubborn and doing it myself and I stumbled and fell down time and time again. I would not accept the idea of asking for help until I wanted to, and I pray that every one of you is able to get to the point where you decide that you WANT it. Go ahead and try doing it on your own first if you have to (just like I did), but I hope that you will be open to wanting it one day. There is so much help and support available to you, but you have to be open to asking for it.

The people that try to be there for you... LET THEM IN. It is so much easier when you have a support system to lean on. You need the people that will see you at rock bottom and not turn their backs on you. Even though you hate letting them see you so weak and vulnerable, let them see you. I know I am just a 28 year old recovering alcoholic and I don't know everything there is to know yet, but I pray that you will not give up in the fight. THERE IS HOPE. THERE IS LOVE. BE OPEN TO IT.

I started writing this book in January of 2017, and I told my therapist in the beginning of March that I wanted to at least put it out as an ebook on the day I would hit my two year anniversary of sobriety. I gave myself a deadline, and about two months to finish the whole thing. I knew I could take my time and try to make it as perfect as possible, but I didn't want it to be perfect. NOTHING about my story is perfect, so I don't intend for my book to be that way either.

I wanted to spend those solid two months pouring everything out exactly as it came out of my heart, and give others the rawest look into what I had gone through and how I had come out of it. There is no way to sugar coat the fact that I had been a hot mess. I had to deal with my own shit. I came out of it stronger. There was no silver lining I could add to the bad times to make them sound better, because the bad times are going to suck no matter how you try to polish them. I wanted to put it out in the most real way possible, so that others could get the most unedited view into my reality.

No two people's relationship with alcohol is the same… so if any part of my story doesn't fit into yours, we've just walked different paths. This is my story, but I hope it has helped you. Remember, YOU ARE NOT ALONE, AND YOU NEVER WERE. You can change your life for the better. The best years are ahead of you, you just have to get there.

BIG THANKS

There are many people I would like to thank and I will probably forget someone in here... So first, to that person I will surely forget to include, THANK YOU.

To my mama, I can never thank you enough. I gave you an entire chapter in my first book, and that doesn't even come close to what I owe you for everything that you have done for me. You have been my rock, my mentor, my mother, my partner in crime, and my best friend. We have laughed until we have cried, and cried until we have laughed. No matter what happens in life, you will always be my everything. I LOVE YOU! (Love, Sassy)

To my entire family: I know I have been a royal pain in the ass. Thank you for never completely turning your backs on me. I know I was a handful and disappointed you along the way sometimes. Thank you for always giving me another chance. Thank you for always being my family and being there no matter what.

To my girl gang, THANK YOU for being my tribe. You have been there for me through thick and thin and I can't thank you enough for that. You have supported me in my crazy ideas and you have been my biggest cheerleaders along the way. I won't be listing all of your names in here because there are far too many people to name. Each one of you know who you are, and I love each and every one of you like the sisters I never had. MUAH!

To the people that have hurt me, lied to me, abandoned me…

You know who you are. Thank you. I will hold on to the good times we shared, but ultimately it is time to let those people and those negative feelings go. I have chosen to forgive them and also free myself from grudges. Thank you for offering me the opportunities to grow and get stronger as a person. Thank you for the lessons. Thank you for the knowledge along the way.

To my therapist Debbie, you have changed my life so much! Thank you for being so welcoming and making my mental and emotional journey so much easier. Thank you for being the biggest supporter of my writing this book! Your encouragement gave me the push to try something way out of my comfort zone, and it has been nothing short of incredible.

To Cara Alwill Leyba, where do I even start? Thank you for being the words I needed to hear when I was in dark times. Thank you for emailing supportive words and advice when I didn't know the first thing about writing a book and was feeling so overwhelmed. Thank you for all that you do to uplift and inspire women around the world. You are making more of a difference in our lives than you could ever imagine. You even inspired me to write a damn book! I know I speak for all of us when I say that you are amazing and we are so thankful for YOU!

To Cara Lockwood and Caroline Johnson, thank you for your beautiful editing and cover designs! I was going into this book totally blind and the two of you helped me to bring it to life! I appreciate your hard work, collaboration, and working with my crazy short timeline to get this released by my special date! You truly helped me turn my baby into something real and amazing.

Thank you to YOU. That's right... YOU, the person reading this book. Thank you for taking the time to read my story. I hope you enjoyed being a part of my journey, and I hope you can pass this along to someone else that might enjoy it too. Thank you for proving my ego wrong when it tried to convince me that nobody would want to read this. Thank you for being a part of one of the biggest accomplishments thus far in my life. You the real MVP.

ABOUT THE AUTHOR

As an entrepreneur, makeup artist, YouTuber, and the creator of *soberAF.com*, Sarah Ordo is your not-so-average female Millennial craving to leave her mark on this world in more ways than one. Her award-winning on location hair and makeup company (based out of Metro Detroit), 24Luxe Hair & Makeup, has been making clients and brides look absolutely stunning for their special occasions since 2013. Her YouTube channel and Instagram page reach thousands of beauty lovers daily featuring the newest trends in makeup, health and fitness tips, and traveling vlogs. She also does a video series on her YouTube channel called *"Let's Talk About"* where she addresses things like self confidence, female empowerment, and mental health issues. Her Youtube videos documenting and following her sobriety have reached thousands of viewers, and have even been featured on *Dateline NBC*.

Sarah's first blog *soberAF.com* has become a place for those on their own journey in sobriety to come together to gain hope and encouragement while connecting with others. She writes about starting her journey in sobriety, living sober, and how to practice self love. *Sober as F**** is the first full-length memoir and book written by Sarah, being released in May 2017. She is currently working on her second book.

Follow Sarah:
www.soberAF.com
Youtube: Sarah Ordo
Instagram: @24Luxe_Sarah

Made in the USA
Middletown, DE
09 April 2018